Property Entrepreneur

Property Entrepreneur

THE WEALTH DRAGON WAY TO BUILD A SUCCESSFUL PROPERTY BUSINESS

Vincent Wong

Registered office
John Wiley & Sons Ltd, The Atrium, Southern Gate, Chichester, West Sussex, PO19 8SQ,
United Kingdom

For details of our global editorial offices, for customer services and for information about
how to apply for permission to reuse the copyright material in this book please see our
website at www.wiley.com.

Library of Congress Cataloging-in-Publication Data is available

A catalogue record for this book is available from the British Library.

ISBN 978-1-119-32640-3 (pbk) ISBN 978-1-119-32642-7 (ebk)
ISBN 978-1-119-32750-9 (ebk) ISBN 978-1-119-32751-6 (ebk)

Cover Design: Wiley
Cover Image: © retrorocket/Getty Images, Inc.

Set in 11/13pt NewBaskervilleStd by Aptara Inc., New Delhi, India
Printed in Great Britain by TJ International Ltd, Padstow, Cornwall, UK

For my father, who entrusted me with representing him on my first ever business trip and inspired me to follow in his footsteps.

Contents

Part III **The Real Deal**

Preface

Whether you've been investing in property for years, or you are a complete newbie, eager to learn and frustrated by not having the money or credentials to get on the property ladder in the traditional way, this book contains some of the most important information you need to know. I wanted to write this book because, when it comes to finding and buying property, I have a wealth of knowledge I want to share. The methods I will be discussing are not those generally talked about. Why? Because none of them benefit the middlemen … the banks, the government and the estate agents! Whether you decide to use any of these methods or not, I believe you have a right to know about them, to have all this information at your disposal.

I think anyone who is serious about investing in today's property market should have access to this information. Everyone deserves to know all the potential options. I'm not suggesting that these new types of property deals are easy, and this is not the "one-size-fits-all" approach that is usually taken in traditional property purchasing. Indeed, some types of deals are only applicable in certain specific circumstances. However, if you want to be in the property *business*, I believe you have to think like an *entrepreneur*. And as an entrepreneur, you need to gather all the information you can lay your hands on so that you can always make an informed *business* decision.

The information in this book is based on all my years and extensive experience in the property business; I believe I have an obligation to share that with you. Every method I describe in detail in this book I have *tried and tested* myself. Knowledge is power and, for too long now, the balance of power has been in the hands of the people who are feeding you information based on what is best for *them*, not *you*. The estate agents, the lawyers, the lawmakers, the government and the media are not thinking of *your* best interests when they advise you, no matter how they dress it up. Do not let them convince you otherwise! *My* advice, to anyone on any issue is get informed, and then make the best decision for *YOU*!

I hope you enjoy this book, I look forward to meeting some of you some day and I wish you all the best on your journey through the property business!

Acknowledgments

I am indebted to so many people for helping to make this book happen. Firstly, thanks to everyone at John Wiley & Sons, especially Thomas Hyrkiel, Jeremy Chia, Gladys Ganaden, Tessa Allen and Caroline McPherson. Thanks also to Miranda Leslau for all her ongoing hard work and expertise in PR. My deep gratitude goes to my family and friends, for your love and support. I wouldn't be where I am today without the support and guidance of all my mentors; your wisdom has helped me become a proud mentor to others who are starting out or re-establishing their property businesses. We all learn from each other; the learning process never stops. I want to thank everyone who works within my property team for helping to run a smooth and successful business, especially my Dutch partner and dear friend, Marina de Haan, and my sister, Florence, for expertly doing so many deals on my behalf. But mostly I am hugely grateful to all the sellers who have ever put their trust in me; whether or not we made a deal, we worked tirelessly together towards a win-win situation. I am always honoured and often humbled to learn about your lives and the circumstances under which you become motivated sellers. You are the ones who drive my passion for the property business ... which, for me, will always be a *people* business.

About the Author

Vincent Wong is co-founder and Executive Chairman of Wealth Dragons Plc. An internationally recognized and respected property entrepreneur, Vincent has generated over 100,000 motivated seller leads to date and has helped hundreds of investors acquire properties with little or no money down. In addition to building his own multimillion pound property portfolio, Vincent has taught deal-making strategies, including lease-option deals – on which he is a world-renowned expert – to investors throughout the world. As an internationally-recognized public speaker and expert in the property industry, Vincent is regularly invited to speak to audiences of 1,000+ delegates at the prestigious Property Outlook Conference in Kuala Lumpur (the biggest property conference in Asia). Vincent is a graduate of The University of London's School of Pharmacy and holds an MBA from Cass Business School.

Introduction: My Property Journey

The first flat I bought was a beautiful Victorian conversion. It was a one-bedroom garden flat in Clapham, in south London, and I paid £73,000 for it in early 1998. At that time I was working as a pharmacist and earning around £32,000 a year, so the flat cost just over twice my annual salary. To put this into context, a similar flat in Clapham now, at the time of writing (February 2016), would cost you upwards of £500,000 and the *top* pay rate for a pharmacist is around £55,000; so, while the top pay for a pharmacist probably hasn't even doubled, property prices have more than quadrupled; the price of that Clapham flat is almost *ten times* what a pharmacist can earn today. This is a staggering gulf and does make you wonder who on earth can afford to buy property in London these days!

Of course, I bought my flat at the bottom of the market and we were about to watch prices soar like never before. Indeed, when I decided to sell the flat in 1999 in order to finance a business idea I'd had, I made a total profit of £36,000. The impact of making so much money in such a short space of time stayed with me and resonated with me for a long time.

For a while my life was full of ups and downs. I trained and worked as a pharmacist and, while I enjoyed the contact with customers and felt I had a good "bedside manner", I'd become frustrated with the glass ceiling in terms of pay. I had decided to study for an MBA, believing it would be my ticket into a fancy high-paid city job. However, I'd failed to get so much as a second interview for a single job. "Overqualified and under-experienced" was how I was described over and over again. My next move was to set up a website. This was during the height of the dot-com boom and I seriously believed I was going to make millions from it. The idea was great; it was a dating website for Asian people. I thought I'd have a huge market considering the population of China and how difficult I assumed it must be for men and women to meet. However, I'd failed to take into consideration the fact that China was way behind the Western world in terms of the Internet and, in reality, my potential customers had no way of using my service. I had to close it down with losses of over £300,000, and to make matters worse, I'd raised all that money through my parents and parents' friends, i.e. within a very close-knit Chinese community – not the most forgiving of people when it comes to losing face!

Finally I sat down and looked at everything I'd experienced. It was like seeing the pieces of a jigsaw finally come together in the right order. I merged the results of all my experiences together and finally made sense of them. First of all I noted that the most money I'd ever made was not by working a set number of hours for anyone (myself or an employer); it was by buying and selling property at the right time. Secondly, although my website had failed because I didn't have the customers to populate it, I knew it had been a good site and I'd gained a great deal of experience in developing it; given the right product and audience, I was sure I could still have a successful Internet-based business. Finally I thought about what a good "people person" I had learnt to be, after all my days working in the pharmacy business. What if, I thought to myself, I could build a website to help people sell their houses quickly and without hassle by connecting them to investors. And thus my business idea for NetworkProperty-Buyers.co.uk was born. I later went on to build NetworkPropertyIn-vestments.co.uk to attract investors for the sellers.

My website was a database of property leads. I basically "match-made" investors and sellers who were particularly motivated to sell their properties. People were able to make direct deals, cutting out the estate agent middleman. Of course, these deals were struck at a lower price than the seller might have received on the open market with an estate agent pushing up the price, but they gladly paid that price for a direct and fast sale. These were people for whom a quick sale, for whatever reason, was paramount.

As the business grew, I began to build my own property portfolio by making deals with some of the leads I found. I also started to come up with more and more inventive ways of doing property deals, so much so that my name became quite well known in the property business and I was sought after by various organizations to speak at conferences and teach what I knew to other property investors. I'll never forget the moment I believed I'd *really* made it; it was when the BBC asked me for an interview. The BBC wanted *my* opinion. I was understandably flattered!

My Property Business Niche

I think I was the first person to hone in on Below Market Value (BMV) deals, and actually systemize the process. Nowadays everyone knows about BMV deals, but back then no one had heard of them. I used my networking skills to find cash-rich investors who were looking for property deals; then I used my marketing skills to find the people who were particularly keen to sell their properties quickly. I introduced them and took a fee for it. In effect I became the middleman myself, but I took my cut from the investor, not the seller. And the sellers always got what they most wanted: a quick sale.

In the couple of years before the Global Economic Crash of 2008/09, my business was booming. I had really carved out a great little niche for myself. However, with my knowledge of economics and general instincts about the way things felt in the property business and other related industries, I could tell a couple of years before the crash happened that the bubble was going to burst, as bubbles always do. We had been watching the subprime mortgage business get quite out of control. It was clearly only a matter of time before it all imploded. In any case, the whole credit/debt culture couldn't last forever. And, unfortunately, the higher you climb, the further you have to fall!

As devastating as the crash was for some people, any savvy entrepreneur knows that in times of economic instability there is always plenty of money to be made. As I saw the crunch coming, I realized that this was going to mean some pretty desperate home owners were going to be needing to offload their properties, some of them might even find themselves in negative equity. The traditional methods of selling through estate agents were not going to help these people, and investors were going to find it harder and harder to get the financing that, to be honest had been a bit of a walk in the park to get up to that point.

This is the Chinese word for crisis:

危机

I love it because it is made up of two characters. The first character means "danger" and the second character means "opportunity".

As the property market started to collapse, I worked harder than ever, coming up with ever-more inventive ways of structuring deals. As a result I, and the many others who followed my lead, survived the crash and actually thrived during these so-called bleak economic times. So I feel I am living proof of the fact that there *is* opportunity within every crisis.

Lease-Option Pioneer

Of all the strategies I have developed to structure property deals, the most pioneering was the lease-option deal structure. Lease-option deals had been used in commercial property but, before I tried it, no one had used such a deal in the purchase of residential property. To me it seemed like a very viable – if unconventional – way of structuring a residential property deal. Working with my lawyers, I set the precedent for using lease-option deals for residential property. I ensured the first deal I did was legally sound and paved the way for any other investor/buyer to use this method.

I like to think I had a small hand in revolutionizing the way property is bought and sold using this particular deal structure! I certainly found myself in great demand after I'd started using this method regularly. People came to me, eager to learn how to structure deals this way. It was a method that allowed me, and many other investors, to carry on investing in property through the credit crunch because it cut out the need for a conventional mortgage. I was soon being invited to speak at international property conferences and receiving more requests for interviews from national television channels. I have continued to teach my unique methods (including lease-option deals and others) to this day, and these strategies form the heart of this book.

Property Revolution

If you can read this book with an open mind, if you can put aside all your preconditioned thoughts about property – what your parents told you, what your bank manager told you, what estate agents have told you – then you stand a good chance of becoming a highly-successful property entrepreneur. This book will change the way you think about property forever.

I believe we are on the brink of a **property revolution**. All the goalposts have moved. Nothing is as it was, and nothing will stay the same as we move forward. The way people own, sell and buy property in the digital age is fundamentally changing. You must expand your thinking; you must keep up with all the relevant government legislation because it will change in the blink of an eye. These days you must be on your toes, you must be adaptable. In many ways it's harder than ever to be successful in the property business, but if you stick with it, you keep learning and you stay flexible, the rewards are *better than ever.*

A Unique Property Book

Books on property investing are literally two-a-penny. You have probably read some of them, as have I. Indeed, if you are serious about being a property investor, you *should* read some of these books to give you a foundation of knowledge, especially if you're completely new to the game. But, no matter what you've read in the past, you've never read a book like this before. Because there isn't one!

What you *won't* be reading in this book is how to manage your property as a landlord, a comparison of available mortgage products, specific tax laws or regulations about buying and selling property related to specific countries or time periods.

What you *will* be reading about in this book is:

1. How to make money from property in any market condition, i.e. regardless of how the economy is doing.

2. How to get into the property business if you don't have the money for a traditional deposit or the credentials to qualify for a mortgage.

Again, I want to emphasize that, apart from a couple of exceptions that I clearly point out, **I have direct experience of every single strategy I outline in this book**. What I'm teaching you is not theory but *practical solutions* so that you can physically go and use these strategies. In most cases I would advise you to learn alongside someone practised in these methods, but there are no barriers to entry. The information is available to you; run with it!

I started my property business with next to nothing, and you can too. The secret to my success is that I've learnt to think outside of the box. That's what every successful entrepreneur has had to do!

Whoever you are, whatever background you are coming from, I hope you learn a great deal from this book. And remember, I want to hear from you and learn from you. I am still on my journey. I never stop learning. I sometimes feel my students teach me as much as I teach them in the long run. So, stay in touch and let me know how you're getting along. The property world is your oyster; don't let anyone else tell you otherwise!

PART

I

THE OLD DEAL

1

The History Of Property

Land ownership has always been a complex and complicated issue. The history of organized land ownership in England really started with the Domesday Book, established in 1086 during the reign of William the Conqueror. This publication was an extensive list of all landholders that outlined all the taxes they owed to the King, who technically *owned* all the land in England. Under the feudal system, lords controlled their allotted land and granted rights to vassals and serfs who could live on and work the land in exchange for allegiance to the lord (i.e. the promise that they would fight to defend their lord if he came under attack in any way, as well as the obligation to serve that lord in whichever way he pleased). Basically it was a form of slavery; those in service to the lord had few rights.

The English Civil War, that saw Charles I executed and the establishment of the Commonwealth under Oliver Cromwell, also brought about the formal end of feudal land tenure. Even after the restoration of the monarchy, it was established (and has been held ever since) that the English monarch could only govern with the consent of Parliament. And thus began common law and the democracy under which we live today.

So what did this mean for land law?

Basically, it led to the establishment of "**freeholders**" of land. The monarch became formally obliged to acknowledge your land rights, i.e. your right to live on the land you "own" as long as you paid your taxes due. From this point, as a freeholder, you were entitled to live on your land free from the obligation of "serving" your lord. Basically you owned the "estate" (which is where the term "real estate" comes from) as opposed to the land, and you were entitled to sell that real estate or pass it on to your heirs. By contrast, **leaseholders** were limited to "owning" the estate for a given lease term, paying a rent to the owner of the land. Typically lease lengths were extensive and these days are usually around 99 years. (In modern times lease-hold properties have become increasingly common where multiple dwellings exist on the same piece of land; for example, purpose-built blocks of flats. If you have 50 flats within a building, it would be a logistical nightmare for all the "owners" to share the freehold, so one landlord usually owns the land and leases it to the owners. If you've ever bought a leasehold flat you'll know that you have to pay "ground rent" to the freeholder, even though you technically own your flat. At the end of a lease, the legal deeds to the property pass back to the freeholder, which is why you should always seriously consider the length of a lease before buying property!)

Common law aside, it was still a long time before ordinary people could buy and sell property because most land was still "owned" by the ruling classes. The working classes still lived in privately owned accommodation and then paid rent to their landlord.

Ownership and Control

The above is an extremely abbreviated account of how property works and scholarly historians would probably baulk at its simplicity, but my objective is to get you to understand what I call the **MYTH OF OWNERSHIP**. Whether we are talking about the land that you "own" – on which you still pay a tax to Her Majesty's Government for the right to live on – or the house you live in – which you prob-ably have a sizeable mortgage on – you do not physically have total ownership of your land.

What you *do* have, to an extent, is **CONTROL**. But even then you are limited. If you want to add an extension to your property, or turn your front garden into a driveway, you must ask permission from the local government. If you live in a listed property, you may have further restrictions on what you can do inside. If there is a seventeenth-century oak staircase in your Grade II listed fourteenth-century manor house, chances are you can't just rip it out and replace it with a modern glass and steel version!

Many people who are in rented accommodation long for their own place specifically because they want more *control*. They imagine how good it will feel when they can paint the living room to their taste, or install a new power shower, without always having to go to their landlord to ask permission. And buying rather than renting your property *does* give you a huge increase in control. You can more or less decorate as you like, and as long as you keep paying your mortgage you can stay in your property for as long as you like without the threat of eviction ... you basically have more *rights*. But it's all still relative.

Remember this concept of **CONTROL** rather than **OWNERSHIP** as it will really help you to understand some of the concepts and "buying" strategies in future chapters.

Modern Land Law

The big reforms in land law in England took place during the late nineteenth and early twentieth centuries. These reforms, both in terms of their fiscal and social implications, widened the scope of ownership and control of property. For example, the Naturalization Act of 1870 gave aliens the right to own and transfer land in England for the first time. The Housing Act of 1919 gave rise to the building of new homes. Many of these first dwellings were built under a scheme called "Homes fit for Heroes" after the First World War. This started a long tradition of building state-owned housing in England, which gave rise to the many council estates that still stand today.

As the demand for social housing grew after the Second World War left over 1.4 million people homeless in England's major cities, new initiatives were started, and eventually the first New Towns Act of 1946 led to the establishment of whole new communities. Entire towns, with all the necessary infrastructure and facilities, were planned. Places like Milton Keynes, Telford, Harlow and Basildon were planned from scratch to cope with the impact of the post-war population boom.

The strain of owning and managing such a large housing stock put huge pressure on local government. In general, the 1960s and 1970s in the UK were years of massive economic unrest and instability. The pound was devalued, economic decline led to trade union strikes and unemployment rose dramatically. The welfare state was stretched and local government coffers were running dry.

Margaret Thatcher's solution, when she became Prime Minister in 1979, was dramatic. She implemented widespread deregulation and privatization in order to boost the economy and undermine the powers of the unions. But by far the greatest impact on the UK's property market came with the Housing Act of 1980, which gave council tenants the "legal right to buy their homes". Tenants were entitled to apply for a mortgage from their local authority. At this time, mortgage interest relief at source (MIRAS) was also in effect, allowing people a certain amount of tax relief on the interest payments on their mortgage. A subsequent act dealt with the problems that many new homeowners faced due to the substandard quality of housing stock. The Housing Defects Act of 1984 gave former council tenants who had unsuspectingly bought their homes only to find major structural problems, the right to apply for local authority grants.

A key feature of the Housing Act 1980 was that council tenants **could pay a deposit of £100 for the right to buy their home at a fixed price for the following two years. If the tenant then went on to sell that house within five years of purchasing it, they had to share the capital gain with the local authority**. (Remember this feature when we come on to talk about options!)

But it was the Housing Act 1988 that brought about the most significant shift of control in favour of private landlords.

Assured Shorthold Tenancy

Until the Housing Act 1988, tenants had significant rights in the properties they rented. If they continued to pay the rent, they couldn't be evicted. But if they didn't pay the rent, it was difficult to evict them.

The Assured Shorthold Tenancy gave landlords the right to give tenants two months notice to leave the property (after the first six months of the tenancy). This differs significantly from the Assured Tenancy, which gave the tenants the right to remain in the property unless the landlord was able to obtain an Order of Possession to evict the tenants. Any rent increases were also subject to review by a Rent Assessment Committee, as opposed to the ability, under the Assured Shorthold Tenancy agreement, of landlords to make whatever rent increases they want (although a tenant does have a legal right to challenge any increase they deem unreasonable).

Obviously, most landlords chose to use the Assured Shorthold Tenancy agreement, even though this often meant a high turnover of tenants. Again, remember this point for later, when we come on to discuss tenant responsibility.

Leases

Although this may seem like it should come before discussion of the Assured and Assured Shorthold tenancies, I've left it until last because it's the most significant concept I want you to remember. It will help you to understand the rest of this book, because it underpins many of the strategies I will be discussing.

Any tenancy is, by nature, a lease. A lease is simply a contractual agreement that is made between a lessor (the legal owner of an asset) and a lessee, which grants rights to the lessee to use that asset. Significantly, **the terms of a lease can be whatever the lessor and lessee agree on**. You could lease someone a tangible asset (such as a car, a phone or a property) or an intangible asset (such as a licence to use a software program or a radio frequency).

You can agree on a fixed-term lease or a periodic lease. You can agree that rental payments are to be made weekly, monthly or annually. But whatever you decide and agree on is fixed. You cannot change the terms of the lease unless both parties are willing to make a new agreement.

When a landlord and rental tenant sign an Assured Shorthold Tenancy (AST) agreement, they are bound by the terms of that standard agreement. *But no one is obliged to offer or accept this type of agreement.* Again, remember this … it will become significant anon!

Playing Monopoly For Real!

In the 1980s and 1990s, private ownership of property sky-rocketed. The rise of the "professional landlord" was a hot topic, and lenders even introduced the "buy-to-let" mortgage in 1996. Being in the property business as all this was happening, as investors were snapping up properties left, right and centre, must have been like seeing a game of Monopoly come to life! The recession of the early 1990s only gave savvy investors the ability to snap up more properties at reduced prices.

New Labour capitalized on the economic strength of Conservative policies while promising better management of spending. When Tony Blair took over as Prime Minister in 1997, the country was already fast climbing out of recession – indeed the economy grew fairly steadily until the big crash that began at the end of 2007, which was precipitated by the undermining of real assets by the subprime mortgage market.

The Aftermath

The aftermath of the global financial crisis was ugly in the property investment world. The collapse of some of the world's biggest banks and financial institutions, such as Lehman Brothers, and major US mortgage companies (Fannie Mae and Freddie Mac), completely destabilized the global economy.

Until this point, we had seen years of hay-making for property investors, as lenders fell over themselves to offer mortgages at ridiculously low rates; everywhere you looked, people were buying properties at inflated prices (speculating they would rise even further) and taking on huge mortgages. Ordinary people were able to invest in property. Never before in the history of Britain had so many people of every social class been able to own property. Teachers, doctors, window cleaners, plumbers and builders were becoming so-called "property millionaires" alongside the traditional wealthy classes.

The problem was that many investors soon found themselves mortgaged up to the hilt with what turned out to be toxic debts. When the housing market collapsed, many people found themselves trapped in negative equity (meaning that their mortgages became greater than the actual value of their properties). The debts were called in and many properties were repossessed. People learned the hard way that being a "property millionaire on paper" wasn't even worth the sheet of paper!

Put it this way: if you had 10 properties each worth £500,000 before the crash, and you had £100,000 of equity in each, you were, at that point, a "property millionaire" (i.e. you owned £1,000,000 of equity). When the property market crashed and each of your £500,000 properties collapsed in price to £400,000, you were suddenly worth nothing (and with £4 million worth of mortgage debt in your name). If those properties slipped even further down to £350,000 each, you now technically owed the bank £500,000 on top of the mortgage debt, i.e. you were in a **negative equity** situation. In commercial property, the bank does not allow you to be in negative equity (in fact you can only be in mortgaged debt up to an agreed loan-to-value, so you always have to make up the shortfall if the value of the property falls); in residential property, you don't have to give the bank anything as long as you keep servicing the mortgage. If you are unable to pay the mortgage on any property, the bank will repossess your property *and* come after you for any shortfall if they don't recover enough to pay off the entire mortgage; i.e. once they repossess, they can claim any shortfall from you. (NB: This only applies in the UK. In the US they cannot come after you for this shortfall, which is why so many people walked away from properties when they fell into negative equity and were unable to keep servicing the mortgage.) If you owe the bank money, you will end up getting a bad credit rating.

This process happened rapidly and left many people reeling. In fact it might be more accurate to call the "aftermath" a "bloodbath"!

If you want a really eye-opening and fascinating account of what led to the global economic crisis, watch Charles Ferguson's Oscar-winning documentary *Inside Job*. Also, Jacques Peretti's brilliant documentary for the BBC, *The Super-Rich and Us*, investigates the rise of the "super-rich" as a result of the crisis and challenges the theory of "trickle-down economics".

But what we were left with (after the aftermath) was actually a potential goldmine for any investor left standing. All the people who'd bought their portfolios when the property market was on the rise, i.e. at the "top of the bubble", had ignored the cardinal rule of **value investing** as decreed by the man known as "the most successful investor in the world", Warren Buffett, who said you should always "**buy low, sell high**". It was the savvy investor who *knew* this, that profited in the aftermath of the crisis by scooping up under-valued properties.

Traditional Property Investing

Until recently, everyone seemed to accept that there were only two ways to become a property owner, which in turn was believed to be the necessary first step towards becoming a property investor. Either you inherited property or you applied for a mortgage and bought it yourself.

When you inherit property from an elderly relative, there is a good chance that the mortgage has been paid off and you will own it outright. Even if there is still a mortgage on it, it's likely that the mortgage is small and there's a sizeable chunk of equity in the property. Either way, as long as you make smart decisions, you've got a good chance of becoming a successful property investor … if that's what you want!

In the past, mortgages weren't too hard to get and properties were affordable. Most professional people with a clean credit history could get a mortgage. People were able to save up for a deposit, or some might have had help from their parents. Once you had a deposit, you'd talk to your mortgage broker or lender and, depending on how much you qualified for, you'd go and look for properties in your price range. You might have chosen to buy a property in need of refurbishment and spent your own time doing it up in order to add value to it. You might have chosen to buy a property with more than one bedroom and rented out the other rooms to help you cover your mortgage repayments, becoming a live-in landlord.

The point is, whichever way you got onto the property ladder, it really wasn't too difficult. However, as I will come to show, for most people, this model simply doesn't work anymore.

Before we look at what does and doesn't work, let's look at two important principles that *any* serious property investor needs to understand: the **principle of leverage** and, related to this, the **myth of ownership**.

The Principle of Leverage

The ancient Greek philosopher and mathematician, Archimedes, said, "Give me the place to stand and I shall move the earth". He was demonstrating the principle of leverage by explaining that if you had a long enough lever and a place to put a fulcrum, you could lift the earth.

In other words, if you've got enough leverage, you can do anything! Leverage is about finding the path of least resistance. Finding the place where you can put in the minimum effort to get out the maximum results. Apply this to property and we're talking about how little of your own money you can put in to get the most out (by selling for profit or renting out).

In our daily lives I believe most people don't think nearly enough about leverage. Even when moving furniture around the house, people just go ahead and do it without thinking of the best *way* to do it. They just bend down, pick something up and run the risk of injuring themselves in the process. In the same way, I watch many property investors put their money into property without thinking through all the possible ways in which they could do it. For example, if you bought a house using all cash (whether yours or someone else's) and then you had to put in a lot of your own effort and money, maybe to refurbish it, after which you made a small amount of profit, then that is not good leverage.

Let's look at a real example to show how leverage works. Let's say you have £250,000 in cash to spend. You could buy a property for £250,000 outright. Now let's say that you sell it two years later for £275,000. You've made a profit of £25,000, and that represents a 10% return on your investment over two years. But your entire pot of £250,000 was tied up in that property, unable to be used for any other investment over the time it took for that property to go up in value.

Now let's say that instead of putting in £250,000 of your own cash, you use £200,000 of someone else's money (a loan) and only £50,000 of your money. Again, after two years you sell the property for £275,000, so you've made a profit of £25,000, but this time the profit represents a 50% ROI (return on investment).

If, using your total pot of cash, you invest in five identical properties and make the same profit each time, then you'd end up, after two years, with £125,000 profit (a total 50% ROI). Which would you rather have?!

The point is, the less money you put in up front, the greater the percentage return on your investment: the more *leveraged* your investment is.

The Myth of Ownership

In the example above, obviously if you used all of your £250,000 pot to buy just one house and went with a 10% return on your investment (£25,000) after two years, then you would own that property outright. However, most people would go for the second option. In this case, you would be borrowing £200,000 on each property. Whoever lends you the £200,000 on each property will have their loan secured by the full value of the property. As long as you keep up your loan repayments, you *control* that property; but if you stop paying, the lender can repossess the property and you'll probably lose your deposit (because they are likely to sell it at a breakeven point, or even at a loss, in order to recover their debt quickly).

We have always put a massive emphasis and great importance on homeownership in Britain – it's a big part of our culture – but few people actually own their house outright. As I've shown above, it really doesn't make much sense to do so. Unless you have no income (and even then, think how much income you can *create* by leveraging your assets!) there is no reason to have all your money tied up in one property.

Sadly, what many people did not quite comprehend when they bought properties at the height of the bubble – with huge mortgage payments and very little deposit – was that it only takes a couple of missed payments before the bank can repossess your property. Many people lost their houses after the financial crash because of this. These days the lenders are a little more responsible, and are legally bound to include the words, "Your home is at risk if you don't keep up mortgage payments" in all advertising.

When you "own" a house with a sizeable mortgage on it, what that means is that you have certain rights. You can a) live in the house without the threat of eviction, b) do whatever you want to it, with the necessary planning permission if applicable, c) rent it out (with the lender's consent) and d) sell it whenever you want and *benefit from the appreciation* (i.e. you own any equity in it over and above what you owe on the mortgage). You see how this is only a step above renting. You simply have more control. You do not "own" the property outright, you are just entitled to live in it and use it more or less how you wish, as long as you keep up your part of the *agreement* (i.e. your repayments) with the lender.

So, keep in mind here that the *key* factors are that you have **control** and that you can **benefit from the appreciated equity**. If you understand these concepts it will help you grasp the strategies I introduce later in the book. I want you to start thinking about property investment in different terms. Instead of thinking about property investment as about *owning* as much of a property as possible, think of it in terms of **gaining the most control and the right to benefit from appreciation for the least amount of money**. The less money you put in, the more leveraged your investment. So, now imagine a situation where you put very little money – even no money – into the property, but still get to control the property and benefit from its appreciation. How good does that sound? Too good to be true? It's not! Stay with me. All will be revealed!

The famous American businessman, John Rockefeller, said: "The secret to success is to own nothing, but control everything."

Learning how to control assets is probably the single most important thing a property entrepreneur will ever learn how to do.

CHAPTER

3

Who Wants To Be A Property Investor?

During my years in the property business, I've met countless investors (and would-be investors) and have identified eight different types.

The Novice

This is one of the *would-be* investors. The "novice" is someone who is looking to get onto the property ladder. They are probably living at home, or renting, with the big dream of being a homeowner motivating them to save for a deposit. Most people don't realize that when they become a homeowner, they are also – by default – becoming a property investor. As such, they should learn everything they can about property investment as many of the same rules apply whether you are purchasing a property as a home or as a rental property. Your home is your biggest investment so you don't want to make any bad choices.

People who are renting are always the keenest to get onto the property ladder. They are painfully aware that rent is dead money and look on enviously as the property market goes up, knowing that they are not benefiting from it. They also know that their situation is always precarious.

As I explained before, the Assured Shorthold Tenancy agreement basically gives landlords the right to serve two months' notice to their tenants at any time (bar the first six months of the contract). In other countries, tenants have far more rights. In many places, as long as the tenant keeps paying the rent, it is very hard to get them out. However, in Britain, tenants live in fear of being given notice. Added to this stress is the knowledge that they cannot control their own property. If they want to paint or put up shelving, they need to ask permission. They may have to wait for repairs to be carried out. Even if you have a great landlord, being a tenant on an Assured Shorthold Tenancy agreement is the least desirable position to be in, in terms of investing for your future.

Most renters are not property owners for one of two reasons. Either they don't buy because they can't get a mortgage (because they have a bad credit history or no credit history), or because they haven't got a deposit saved up. These days, the sad thing is that it is virtually impossible for young people to save up for a deposit in today's market. Both the market and the lending parameters are stacked against them. In the next section, we will look at some figures and see how impossible it is for most young people to get onto the property ladder in the traditional way.

The Homeowner

There is a common expression that says "An Englishman's home is his castle". Initially it was intended to mean that a man may do whatever he pleases in his own home and that no one can enter a person's home without the owner's permission. Of course it was later amended to reflect the fact a man may only do what is *legal* in his own home, and that if a necessary warrant is obtained then law enforcement officers can force entry. But the expression has a wider significance in suggesting every "Englishman" (and woman) aspires to be a homeowner. This was Margaret Thatcher's legacy. She encouraged a culture in Britain that emphasized the goal that everyone should be aspiring to own their own home. The legacy remains as strong as ever today.

In Britain (far more than in other cultures), as soon as you leave college or university, you are advised to get onto the property ladder as quickly as possible. Obviously most people can't afford to buy property outright, using cash. Most people don't have that kind of money to hand, unless they are in a very fortunate bracket. The idea, of course, is that you make money by sitting on your investment while the price of your property goes up. You wait a few years until you have a sizeable chunk of equity in the property, and then you sell and buy a larger property, in effect moving up another rung on the property ladder. You keep doing this until you reach the top of your earning capacity and the biggest property you are ever going to live in. At this point, as your children leave the nest, you might decide to start downsizing. You've probably paid the mortgage off by this time. You can now sell up, buy a smaller place and use some of the equity in your property pot to supplement your pension. Potentially, at the end of your life, you might have some equity left in your property to leave as an inheritance for your children or grandchildren.

There is something quintessentially British about this obsession with owning property at all costs. In many other countries, especially in the cities, people are not as desperate to own their property, they are happy to rent indefinitely. In cities like New York, Paris and Amsterdam particularly, compared to London, people do not seem to feel such an urgent need to live in property that they own. I am certain this is because of our unique Assured Shorthold Tenancy agreement. In other cities, tenants have more rights and thus are happier to rent (often buying, when they can afford to, in more rural locations where they can get far more bang for their buck!).

Of course there are also negatives to owning property, which we will come on to explore later, but the benefits are clear to see.

While there can be a fantastic return on your investment as a homeowner, this is not your first priority, so you're not really behaving like an investor. As a homeowner you want a nice home, so you will spend money on it without thinking about profit. You will spend money to make your home as beautiful and comfortable as you can make it. You have different motives. As an investor you want to maximize your profit, so you don't want to spend too much money on the property, you want to *make* money on it. Ultimately, you are looking to make a rental income from your property investment.

> **A homeowner uses their income to pay the mortgage.**
> **An investor uses their mortgage to get an income.**

When you are a homeowner, you have to pay your mortgage, out of your salary, every single month. This is why a lot of people want to own their house outright, so that they don't have mortgage payments every month. Ultimately, when you have a mortgage on a property you don't truly own it and, just as a landlord can always serve notice on a renter, the bank has the right to repossess your property if you stop paying your mortgage (and you would have far more to lose than a renter!). Any mortgage comes with very clear warnings that your home is at risk if you do not keep up your mortgage payments on it.

So, people want to pay off their mortgages for two reasons. Firstly, they want to increase their equity in the property, but secondly – and most importantly – they don't want to be at risk from bank repossession. They view their mortgage as a bad debt and try to get free of it as quickly as possible.

(I will come on to explain, in a future chapter, why a mortgage is actually a good debt and it is not the best idea to pay it off as quickly as you can.)

The point that I am making here is that a homeowner is not actually a real investor; however, owning a home is still better than not being on the property ladder at all because at least you are accumulating *some* wealth. Some people believe that being a homeowner is the be all and end all. I'm here to tell you that it's not!

The Academic

These are my least favourite people! These are the people who spend a great deal of time talking about property. They read a lot of books, memorize statistics, throw their opinions around on property forums and generally make a great deal of noise. But it's all based on what they've read, not on what they've experienced. Trust me, no one who is a serious property investor has time to dream up online alter egos and post hundreds of comments a day on property-related threads!

All that these "academics" seem to do is criticize. They are naysayers, spreading doom and gloom to put others off (presumably because they are too negative and cowardly to get out and start actively investing themselves). They love telling people what to do, even though they are doing none of it themselves. I call them property trolls because they are just spreading negativity across various online property sites. Most of them are not investing; they would do *anything* rather than actively invest in property. They do not contribute to the industry in any way, shape or form!

The Developer

These people see value in property only if there is work do be done to it, i.e. if they can force the appreciation of the property by raising its value even without a move in the market. This type of investing became very popular as a result of TV shows such as *Property Ladder* and *Homes Under the Hammer*. It's all about developing and refurbishing a property. We see people in these TV shows who buy a property at auction that's in a bad state of repair; they completely renovate the property and then sell it on for a profit (or sometimes keep it to rent it out to give them a passive income). The people who do best out of this type of investing are builders, because they can do the work themselves. The people at greatest risk are those who are not builders and have absolutely no experience of commissioning building work, because they are usually unaware of how quickly budgets can spiral and profits can disappear!

Often these properties are in such a bad state of repair they are literally unmortgageable. However, a lender will usually give you a chance to bring it up to standard. If you can get a bridging loan (or, as a successful developer, can bankroll your project) allowing you to finance the purchase and the renovation work, the lender will give you a guarantee that if you meet certain criteria and complete the agreed list of repairs then they will lend you the mortgage. Basically, a surveyor's report can come back with a "full retention" recommendation, i.e. the surveyor does not recommend that a mortgage is offered on the property at all (a specific value is not put on the property), or a "partial retention" recommendation, which is where a surveyor will suggest a value subject to a specific list of works being carried out satisfactorily. Once the work is done, the developer's exit strategy will either be to sell it or to refinance it according to the terms that the lender offered.

The people who got it right (made good property choices that didn't have any hidden horrors and kept to their budgets) made a fortune doing this. The TV shows inspired ordinary people to become property developers. People gave up their day jobs to become property developers. The point was, anyone could do it: teachers, nurses, civil servants … anyone. And once people got a taste for how much money they could make developing property, they didn't want to work in nine-to-five jobs earning limited salaries.

For a while, property development was almost foolproof. Those who did well made a substantial amount of money; but those who did a bad job on their property and ran way over budget *still* made money. I remember watching one of Sarah Beeny's programmes and the couple had done a terrible job on their renovation. They'd made some disastrous choices and had run severely over budget. However, they didn't lose any money because the market had gone up so much in the time it had taken them to do the renovation that the increase in their equity in the property on top of the forced appreciation from the renovations actually covered their costs. However, as Sarah Beeny pointed out, they would have done better just to have flipped the property without doing the work. Then at least they would have made a greater profit rather than spending all that money on renovations. They really did waste a lot of cash.

This, of course, was all prior to 2008, when we kept seeing massive jumps in the property market as we were approaching the property bubble (that eventually burst!). During this time, the market was very forgiving of mistakes. In a way, this is what made the crash even more painful, and why I call it something of a bloodbath. As the market began to collapse it became a total buyers' market. Many developers, who had sunk a huge amount of their own money or borrowed money into their developments, were unable to sell because they couldn't even recover their costs. Their cash was all locked up in developments that had been bought at totally inflated prices. Then matters got worse as they discovered they couldn't even service the debts on their properties. If any of those properties had mortgages on them, the developers ran the risk of losing everything, because banks have a definite deadline on when loans must be paid back. If you miss the deadline, the property will be repossessed.

I also came across many developers during these post-crash years who were highly "geared", which means that they owed huge sums of money in loans, and to whom the banks' surveyors had returned full or partial retention orders on properties. However, when the work was completed, the banks reneged on their promises and the developers were unable to get the properties financed. It became a sad and common occurrence during these times to hear of banks suddenly withdrawing mortgage offers at the last minute. They always ensured they had the right to … it was all in the small print! Even right up to the last minute they could pull an offer, and people on the verge of completion had the rug pulled out from under them. During the credit crunch, the banks discovered that their mortgage books were way too big, so they were looking for all and any excuses not to lend.

Another symptom of the credit crunch was that the banks would instruct their valuers to be extremely cautious, even to down-value properties. So for some developers, even if they could get the bank to go through with the loan, the size of it was so reduced that they might not be able to break even on their investment.

Many professional developers, such as building companies, were public companies and were well capitalized, so they were able to ride out the storm. When times were bad, they could afford to leave developments unfinished and complete them further down the line (these developers are now doing very well again). However, for the average Joe who had got into developing on a whim and because it had gone so well initially in a booming market, the credit crunch years were a terrible blow. The experience highlighted how risky the whole game can be. The idea of taking on a refurbishment with limited resources carries huge risk, especially when the building industry itself is so unregulated. There are more forums for swapping stories about building companies now, but it's still not an efficient market, you really don't know what you are dealing with unless you have a lot of experience. You can easily find yourself over budget, out of time or ripped off. I've seen people go bankrupt as a result of their inexperience, people with large portfolios that got repossessed.

A developer is not necessarily the smartest investor, unless they really know what they are doing.

The Speculator

A speculator is someone who buys a house in a particular area that they believe will go up in value. They identify hotspots, perhaps because of a new transport link or major shopping centre being built. When the Crossrail project was announced, people at the end of the line in Essex saw their properties increase in value because of the future fast link to London's Heathrow airport.

Sometimes, of course, the project doesn't actually happen. Councils love to announce that they are building new facilities (a new leisure centre perhaps) and then end up delaying for years. Or Sainsbury's will announce a new hypermarket and, after a couple of years, pull out. Starbucks used to be a good guide for gauging where a new property hotspot was going to spring up. People would "follow the Starbucks sign" into new areas. If there was a new Starbucks being built in an area, or a new Tesco Metro, then a mini boom would be expected.

But no one can tell you for certain whether one area is going to go up in price more than any other.

I remember an area near Milton Keynes where a big new Sainsbury's was planned. House prices went up for a while. However, for whatever reason, Sainsbury's decided to relocate. They pulled out and that big building remained vacant for a considerable amount of time. House prices became stagnant thereafter.

People often approach me and ask me where is a good place to buy. I always say, "I don't know". There are no guarantees; for that you would literally need a crystal ball. The media often makes predictions on where the next big property hotspot is going to be. Sometimes they will get it right, but there are still never any *guarantees.*

Another type of speculator is someone who buys properties off plan from the developers. There was a time, pre-crisis, when this was highly popular. For example, a developer would buy land and make plans to build an apartment building on that land. To help finance the development, they would get a load of property speculators to put down deposits on apartments at a "discounted" price. For the speculators this seemed like a great way of making a long-term profit. The development would normally happen in three or four phases, the first of which would literally just be sketched. The earlier the phase at which you invested, the greater the "discount" you would receive. (I write "discount" because – as I will come on to explain – these prices were highly inflated in the first place so the discount was rather misleading.) The developer would often hold onto some of the apartments in order to sell them at higher prices later, when the market would also have gone up.

The speculator in this scenario would make their money not only through the upturn in the market, but also because they had initially bought their property at a so-called discount.

But there was a flaw in the plan.

When speculators bought at the planning stage, obviously they just put down the deposit and exchanged contracts. What they were hoping to do was to complete just before the development was finished, and they were obliged to complete so that they could release their profit without ever having to go through the competition stage (by simply signing it over to the new owner and allowing their money to pay off the original developer). Speculators with a large lump sum would actually try to put down deposits on as many units as possible to maximize their potential profit (and also because the developer would usually give you an even bigger discount if you bought in bulk). At this point, the speculator is taking all the risk because he is obliged to complete, even though all he has done at this point is exchange contracts. The speculator is now at risk in two ways. Firstly, if the developer goes bankrupt (which pre-crisis was highly unlikely, but post-crisis was happening all the time) the bank will repossess the whole development and the speculator loses his deposit. Secondly, if there is no buyer for the apartment (because buyers can't get the bank to lend at the price the speculator needs to sell for), then the speculator is forced to complete the sale. If the speculator doesn't have the funds to do that, then they will forfeit their right to buy the property and, again, lose their deposit.

There was one further problem that emerged for these poor speculators.

Because the developer often kept back some of the apartments, they were able to offer buyers huge incentives to buy from them. They would offer free furniture or kitchen upgrades, even cash-back offers, to get people to buy. Speculators couldn't compete with that. How could the developers afford to offer these great incentives? Because they had inflated the prices in the first place, so they got themselves into a win-win situation. A property is only ever worth what someone will pay for it, so you can go ahead and name your price and see what happens. Prior to the credit crunch, a lot of developers colluded with lenders who would agree to lend the potential buyer 90–95% of what the developer said it was worth. The lender would give the developer a discreet guarantee that they would value the property at the inflated price. The banks were on the make as much as anyone else. They believed that property prices were going to continue to go up and up. Even if the buyer seemed like a risky borrower, they wouldn't worry too much because they were confident that the increase in the market would easily cover the potential risk.

Many of these types of developments were city centre apartments in places like London, Liverpool, Manchester and Leeds. They made very little sense. In a very similar area, £350,000 would buy you a three-bedroom house with a garden *or* … a two-bedroom flat with a small balcony and a concierge on the front desk. And we are not just talking about 10 or 20 flats here; we're talking developments of 50 to 100, sometimes up to 500 flats.

The property developers knew what they were doing, they weren't really building for the general public, they were building for property speculators, knowing that they could make money that way in the short term. Thus began a vicious circle that could not end well for the speculators.

Here's what would happen.

Say a flat was *valued* at £300,000 and the bank lends the speculator 95% of that. The mortgage is then £285,000. If the interest on that mortgage is 4%, each year that speculator is paying £11,400 in interest alone. That works out at £950 per month (interest only). When you've got 100 or 200 landlords in the same building needing to rent out their properties, what do you think the competition is going to do to the rental prices? Obviously it is going to push rent prices down. It becomes a renters' market in that building. The renter might pay around £600 a month for the property, which won't even cover the speculator's interest. All those speculators started *losing* money (if they were even lucky enough to get tenants) every month!

I remember a particular development in Northampton where loft-style two-bedroom apartments sold for £300,000 each. But they didn't fetch more than £600–700 per month in rent. Any landlord with a large mortgage would have been losing money.

During the boom years, I remember many people were happy to be losing a few hundred pounds every month because they believed the prices would go up so much that they would cover themselves in the long run. Then … BAM! The crisis hit and the property market began to collapse. Now, not only were they losing money every month, but they were hurtling towards their properties being in negative equity, so even if they sold they wouldn't be able to pay the bank back. As speculators fell over each other in desperation to sell, of course this also drove down the prices of these apartments. I will never forget coming across an apartment in 2010 that sold at auction for £80,000. At its highest price the apartment had sold for £300,000!

Some people who held on to these properties, losing thousands and thousands of pounds, came to me to ask if there was anything they could do to recover their losses. Sadly, the answer was always "no".

Even today when people ask me if it's a good idea to buy off plan I advise caution. When these properties crash, they plummet. They are the type of property that is hit hardest by property price dips. The problem is, people don't really live in these types of apartments in England. In London, admittedly, they work a bit better, mostly because of the expat community – people from other countries who are used to apartment living. London kind of has its own climate in that way. But they don't really work in other centres, like Liverpool, Leeds and Manchester. The English like living in houses. We're not an apartment-living nation; we like our gardens and guttering!

But even in London to get into a new build is extremely expensive. So the conclusion is … speculation does not automatically equal investment. Speculation is only based on your personal view of the market. If you ask five different so-called property experts you'll get five different opinions, just as you'd get five different opinions of how the economy is doing if you ask five different economic experts about the growth of the UK economy.

The Fallen Angel

What I call "fallen angels" are those people who were once the big successful rising stars of the property industry but who fell on hard times when the market changed dramatically. In the property boom, before the global financial crash, these people were heavily mortgaged or geared (having secured huge amounts of financing to buy houses or invest in developments) but the massive downturn in the market meant that, suddenly, they were unable to cover their mortgage interest with their rental income. They soon discovered they were losing money every month. Many of them saw their equity disappear as prices plummeted. Some even found their properties went into negative equity.

These "fallen angels" were the direct victims of the crisis. When you've benefited directly from a bubble, you have to accept that your success has been fuelled by debt. When the market tumbles, that debt still has to be serviced, and if you can't keep up your repayments, you're in serious trouble. These people could no longer sustain their portfolios using debt because the credit had dried up. Lenders have tightened the purse strings and are not handing out mortgages (credit) in the way they used to. It has become increasingly hard to get a mortgage.

These people all think it's the end of the road for them, because they have bad credit due to missed repayments, or because they have had their portfolio repossessed. Some of them have even declared bankruptcy. However, they still have their passion; all these people have vast experience in property, they still love property and they know the merits of building wealth through property. That is all highly relevant. All they really need to do is learn new strategies and find new ways to finance their portfolios.

I've seen so many people who believe they have reached the end of the road because they get repossessed or have to declare bankruptcy. They've completely fallen out with the banks and they think they will never be able to invest in property again. I try to encourage them by explaining it is not the end of the road for them. These people are usually highly distressed; they don't know where to turn. They come to me and say things like: "I used to have 30 properties and they were all repossessed … and now I have nothing." Or they explain to me that some of their properties have been taken away and they are struggling to pay the debt on the rest. These people are usually in a wretched situation that has had terrible repercussions on their lives. The stress might have even cost them their marriage. I feel so sorry for them and I always try to help them by explaining that they shouldn't give up.

At the end of the day, I still consider these fallen angels property investors. They often find it very hard to have hope, but I explain that they still have their experience. Everyone hits hard times, most successful entrepreneurs have had several failed businesses; I try to get them to see that they have just had a setback, that they are not completely washed up.

The worst thing I see some of these fallen angels do is sacrifice their cash flow to try and protect their credit records. Their debts pile up and instead of cutting their losses and allowing their properties to be repossessed or filing for bankruptcy, they carry on, month after month, servicing their debts, sometimes shelling out thousands on their debt repayments. This is crazy; it's throwing good money after bad.

At this point, I explain to people that they should think about letting their liabilities go. When a property is *costing* you so much money instead of *making* you money, and there is no other way around it, then it's sometimes a better idea to let it go. But people are terrified of going bankrupt. They convince themselves that it's a good idea to stay in the race because that's the only way they will make a comeback. But this isn't necessarily the best thing to do. If you are using all your income to service your debt, then you are not going anywhere. The suffering is not worth it. These days there are people with perfect credit scores who *still* don't get mortgages, and others who have just missed one or two credit card payments in their lives who don't qualify for mortgages, so why are these poor people sacrificing all their income to protect their credit history when it might not be as valuable as they think?

It really breaks my heart to see people servicing their debts in this way, using every penny of their salary. I always impress upon them that bankruptcy is *not* the end. Many of the most successful businesspeople you see in the media have gone through bankruptcy or insolvency on some of their businesses.

The point I'm trying to make here is that, when it comes to the choice of using all your hard-earned cash to service a debt or filing for bankruptcy, the latter is often the lesser of two evils. You shouldn't sacrifice things like your health, your relationships or your sanity for the sake of not having a bankruptcy on your record. Trying to protect your credit rating by servicing unmanageable amounts of debt is futile. If the situation has got that bad, you need to think bigger – and more strategically. Sometimes it is better to let the bank repossess the house or to declare yourself bankrupt. I am *not* advocating bankruptcy or suggesting people be irresponsible, but it is sometimes a better option than an even more drastic situation.

Most people will do *anything* to avoid bankruptcy, and while I am not suggesting that you reach for bankruptcy lightly, I am saying that it is occasionally the right choice. These days, bankruptcy does not have quite the same stigma as it used to have. You're discharged from bankruptcy after six months and, while it stays on your record for a further six years and prevents you from most ways of getting credit, it does not stop you from operating as a property investor, as I will come on to explain in the final section.

What I'm basically saying is that all is not lost; there are ways to move forward. You can learn how to do property deals without borrowing money.

The Value Investor

In stark contrast to speculators, who mostly buy their property at full market value with a view to seeing the value going up in the future, value investors look for under-valued assets. For example, if the value investor finds a property that is worth £300,000 and then buys it for £200,000, he's made an instant paper profit of £100,000, which is added to his personal net worth. It's called a **Below Market Value Deal** or **BMV Deal**. Whenever I tell people this, they almost always ask, "But is this even possible? How on earth can it be possible?"

Not only is it possible, but I have actually used this method of value investing principles to build my own portfolio.

Value investing is not a new concept, of course. Warren Buffett, one of the richest investors in the world, built his fortune using value investing. He grew his wealth by buying shares in companies trading below their asset value. The stock market, like many markets, is not an efficient market. An efficient market is one where, whenever there is a discrepancy between the price of an asset and its real value, the market will immediately adjust the price. Neither the stock market nor the property market is an efficient market. Value investors in any market always make a better return on their investment in the long run; the secret is knowing where to look!

In his book, *One Up On Wall Street*, the American investor and author, Peter Lynch, outlines a system for identifying share prices that are trading at below the company's real potential net worth.

So, how do we apply value investing to property? How do people find those Below Market Value (BMV) deals?

There are a number of ways in which you can begin to look for BMV deals in property. You should start by understanding that the property business (for the purposes that we are talking about here) is not about the physical properties, it's about the people selling those properties. For every property that is offered for sale, there is a seller with a *reason* for selling it, and not all sellers' reasons are the same. Some sellers' reasons are more urgent than others. If the seller has a definite timeframe in which the property has to be sold (perhaps because it would otherwise be repossessed or because the seller has to move urgently) then that seller might consider selling at below market value in exchange for **certainty** over the sale.

For example, a bank might be selling a property that it has repossessed after the owner stopped paying the mortgage. The bank might consider selling the property at a 20% discount just so that they can quickly recover the loan made on the property. The bank is simply looking to cut its losses and recoup some of the loan it made.

Another example might be a seller who has lost his job and is behind with the mortgage payment. If the property is not sold within a set period of time then it could be repossessed. The seller might be happy to get a guaranteed sale and avoid the repossession order, even if it means losing all their equity in the property by accepting a BMV deal.

Remember that not everyone who is highly motivated to sell is in a so-called "desperate" situation. Some people are simply keen to release equity and move on with their lives, perhaps because the property was an inheritance and they don't want to deal with the maintenance, or they need to split the proceeds between benefactors. It might be because they are keen to emigrate abroad in a certain timeframe. Not everyone wants to wait to sell their property or go through the hassle of dealing with estate agents.

Most people automatically assume that a property is an **asset**. That's what the media always talks about. We see properties as assets. But this is only half the story. Whether the property is an asset or not depends on the property owner's personal circumstances. If the property owner cannot benefit from the property directly, or cannot service the debt secured on it, then the property becomes a **liability**.

When you have a liability, you need to get rid of it as soon as possible!

I will be discussing ways to find sellers who might be interested in making a BMV deal in more detail in a later chapter. The fact is: people who need to sell their properties quickly will need to reduce the price, sometimes quite substantially, to make a quick sale. If a seller needs speed then they know they will probably have to sacrifice the price. It's always possible to find under-valued assets because sellers have different circumstances. That's what makes the market inefficient, sellers always have the choice of dropping their price if they want.

BMV investors have benefited enormously from this inefficient market, as did the banks prior to 2008.

In the past, what happened was this.

Traditionally, when you bought a property, you put down a deposit and the bank paid the rest with the mortgage. So say you wanted to buy a property for £200,000, that meant the bank wanted you to pay a 20% deposit of £40,000 and would give you a mortgage of £160,000. However, say you were able to negotiate the price of the property down to £160,000. Then you would be able to buy the property outright with a quick bridging loan of £160,000. Once the property was in your name, you would refinance it, taking out a mortgage for £160,000, which is an 80% mortgage on the original valuation of £200,000. Now you've got £160,000 in your pocket to pay back the bridging loan and you have in your possession a £200,000 property. You didn't have to put any money down and yet you have £40,000 of equity in the property. People were doing these kinds of deals all the time pre-crash. It's called a "no-money-down deal". Furthermore, if you could get the price of the property down to £150,000, you'd get £10,000 in your pocket, cash back, tax-free. That's like being *paid* to buy a property!

Some investors were able to help out people who wanted to release the equity in their property but remain living in it, in deals that were called "sale and rent-back". On face value, and when conducted by ethical investors, these deals were extremely beneficial to both parties. Say an elderly couple wanted to release the equity in their home but keep living in it; they effectively sold it to an investor and rented it back from him or her. It was a great deal for the investor because it created guaranteed tenants who already loved the property!

Unfortunately, some BMV buyers behaved terribly. As prices went up, they decided to kick the tenants out and sell the property to make a profit, leaving the original owners homeless. This gave a very bad name to "sale and rent-back". As a result this has become a highly regulated area of the property business, and the conditions are so stringent it's not really worth pursuing as an investment tactic anymore.

I have always taken care to work only with a select group of investors: people I trust and I know will behave scrupulously. My main property business is dealing with sellers, so I want to protect the sellers as much as the buyers. Anyone who works with me has to abide by my code of ethics.

I think that some of my concern for people, especially elderly people, comes from the years when I worked as a pharmacist. I used to spend ages talking to the elderly. Ostensibly most of them came in to buy a packet of tissues or a toothbrush, but I knew most of them were there because they were lonely. They came in for a chat. So I do feel rather protective of this group, especially when I see cowboys taking advantage of them, trying to persuade them to sell their properties. Having the ability to buy a property is a powerful position and as Peter Parker (Spiderman) knows … with great power comes great responsibility!

With these lucrative loopholes closing (spoiling things for the more responsible investors), times are even bad for value investors now. I will be discussing this more in the next chapter.

Although it was a good thing that the cowboys were weeded out, it means that the application of BMV deals is not as readily lucrative as it used to be, because you can't technically do a BMV deal with a view to making money through refinancing. Even if you buy for cash and try to refinance six months down the line, the bank will question the sudden increase in valuation. You can only really make money through a BMV deal if you are a) going to flip the property, i.e. buy for cash and then *sell* it on quickly for a profit, or b) if you are going to simply keep the property in your portfolio for a reasonable length of time to make money through rental income.

However, there are still plenty of people who want to be value investors and *do* care about the sellers. I am one of them. Some of us *do* have an ethical approach to value investing in property, and I work with others who share my approach.

I want to share my knowledge to teach others how to be value investors; how to do it ethically and responsibly, while making a profit.

The Dealmaker

This is the new generation of property investors. In today's market, if you truly want to make money in property, you have to learn how to make deals in a way that you probably haven't thought of before.

Remember I explained how the Chinese symbol for "crisis" is the combination of two symbols (one meaning danger and the other meaning opportunity)? Well, here's the opportunity side of the crisis.

We've established the fact that you can't rely on traditional ways of financing property deals and you can't be a cowboy anymore (although hopefully you didn't want to be one in the first place!). So, how do you get financing? Well, there is a whole new breed of investors who are not fazed by the difficulty in getting finance. These people think outside of the box. It doesn't matter what they've done in the past – some of them have even been bankrupt – and they don't care about the constraints in the market, they know that they can still make lucrative property deals. These new investors, these *dealmakers*, find ways of acquiring properties, or building assets and creating cash flow, regardless of their situation. When there are problems, they find solutions.

I call these people the new dealmakers: the property entrepreneurs.

These property entrepreneurs are the new makers and shakers of the property market. They are, first and foremost, dealmakers. Their focus is on providing solutions to the sellers. By helping the sellers, they help themselves. They do win-win deals. They will do whatever it takes as long as it is ethical and legal. They will find the grey areas and walk into them. They will seek out loopholes and use them. When the loopholes get closed, they will find new ones. They never accept that something is "impossible" – they will seek out a way to make the deal work; they will say, "Let's see how we can make this work". It doesn't even matter if you've been bankrupt because dealmakers don't rely on the banks to make their deals.

The very definition of the word *entrepreneur* is someone who takes risks to start new businesses. They take *risks* and they do something *new*. This is exactly what these new property entrepreneurs are doing. They don't view property as a side business or a hobby; property is a serious business for them. However, as entrepreneurs, they don't play by the rules – they create their own rules.

Entrepreneurs solve problems that benefit them and their clients/customers.

As a pioneer of new deal structures for controlling and acquiring property, it is this eighth category that I put myself in and, if you want to be a smart investor, I suggest you put yourself in this category, too. The rest of this book is written *specifically* for people who want to be dealmakers, for people who see themselves as property entrepreneurs.

PART

II

THE NEW DEAL

4

What's Wrong With The Old Deal?

So why do we need a "new deal" at all? Well, because the "old deal" doesn't work anymore. In the last section we looked at the "novice" investor, i.e. the person who is living in rented accommodation or with their parents who desperately wants to get on the property ladder. I said that, these days, it is virtually impossible for a novice to get on the property ladder in the traditional way (i.e. save a deposit and apply for a mortgage from a high street lender). Now let's look at *why* that is.

In 1995, if you were a 25-year-old living in London on a salary of £18,000, you could have easily saved up a deposit of £3,000 over a couple of years (that's about 8% of your gross salary per year). If you'd stayed in your job for more than two years and had a good employer's reference, most lenders would have happily given you a mortgage of around three times your salary (i.e. £54,000) as long as you could put down at least 5% of the value. Thus, with your £3,000 deposit and £54,000 mortgage, you could buy a property for around £57,000 (plus costs). Indeed, anyone fortunate enough to get *on* the property ladder in 1995 saw their properties double in value over the following two or three years. If they kept those properties, even if they saw a dip during the crash, those properties would still be worth today around four times what they were worth 20 years ago.

In 1995, it was possible to buy a small, one-bedroom flat in, say, Zone 3 in London, for £57,000. That same property in today's market is now probably worth around £250,000. That's well over a 300% increase. By comparison, the type of job that commanded a salary of

£18,000 in 1995 would probably pay in the region of around £25,000 today. That's just short of a 40% increase.

You can already see the problem … 40% can't compete with 300%!

In any case, all the rules have changed. These days, banks will only give mortgages of 80–90%. So if you wanted to buy a property worth £250,000, you'd have to save up a minimum of £25,000. But that would assume you've got a salary of £75,000 to qualify for a loan of £225,000 (three times your salary). The young, first-time buyer is more likely to be on a salary of £25,000. After tax on this salary, you are probably taking home around £1,700 a month. Once you've paid your rent, your bills, travel costs and eaten modestly, you'd be lucky to be able to put away £200 a month. At that rate it would take you 125 months (over 10 years!) to save £25,000. At which point, house prices will probably have doubled anyway. If you tried to go down this road, you would always be chasing the market; you would never catch it up. Your only hope would be someone giving you that lump sum as a private loan. And in any case, you would still only be able to borrow three or maybe four times your salary of £25,000 (£75,000–100,000) so if you actually wanted to buy that £250,000 property, you'd need to save at least £150,000. At £200 a month, that would take you 750 months (41 years!) so that makes no sense at all!

So what are wannabe first-time buyers supposed to do?

After crunching the above figures, I think you can see it's almost impossible for most people to get a foot on the property ladder in the traditional way. It's impossible to save enough for a deposit, given current prices, and to keep up with inflation. If you can't get a first property, you can't start your career as a property investor. Whether you are buying your first property as a home or as a starter investment property to rent out, the rules are the same … in fact it's even harder to get a buy-to-let mortgage if you haven't had a mortgage before. You usually can't borrow as much as you can as a homeowner.

If you were a first-time investor, first you'd look for a property that you thought had good rental potential as well as good appreciation potential. You'd look in areas with buoyant rental markets, preferably where demand was still very high because people were constantly moving into the desirable area and because existing tenants in the area were upgrading to larger properties. Once you'd identified the area and found a property you believed had good potential, you'd go to the estate agent listing the property and put in an offer. If the asking price was X, you would put in an offer at X - Y (Y being a certain percentage discount) and hope for the best. If the offer was accepted, you'd at least know you had got a bargain, and potentially made a paper profit, because you'd knocked something off the asking price. Next, you would apply for a mortgage. For a buy-to-let mortgage, the bank would typically loan you around 75% of the value of the property, so you'd have to come up with the 25% deposit. Then both the buyer and seller would instruct their lawyers to conduct the conveyancing (the legal process). When the sale of the property completes, the buyer gets the key, the seller takes the money and moves on, the estate agency and lawyers get their respective commission and fees, and the lender collects the interest every month. Everyone is happy.

If the investor wants to expand their portfolio, they have to wait for the property to go up in value. Then they can go to the lender and say, I want to remortgage in order to release some equity and use it to buy the next house. Of course, now the investor is borrowing much more money from the lender so the interest goes up and, to reflect this, the investor puts the rent up (it's always the tenant who pays the investor's mortgage). By releasing equity as the value of his properties go up, the investor can keep adding to his portfolio. A typical investor, in his lifetime, might acquire a portfolio of around 8 to 10 properties over 20 years or so.

This route hasn't changed, but if the investor can't get onto the ladder in the first place, they can't even get started.

The other problem with the "old deal" is that it pushes prices up into a bubble that will eventually burst.

When an agent puts a property on the market, they put it on at an **asking price**. Obviously market forces come into play and price reflects supply and demand, but the agent will *always* inflate the price of a property when they first put it on the market. They are chancing it; they are seeing what they can get. This is *not* the true value of the property; it is based on the estate agent's motivation a) to get a bigger commission, and b) to push the market up. If estate agents didn't do this, the market would get stagnant. If properties always sold at the same price as the last comparable property, the market would never go up.

An estate agent's primary motive is to get as much as possible for a property. They are not motivated to get a quick sale, or a deal that helps the seller's personal circumstances. In fact, they are not motivated by the seller's needs at all. All the estate agent cares about is getting the highest price for that property and pushing the market up, because both are good for their business. Of course, the more they can get for a property in a certain area, the more they push up the prices of all comparable properties in it. Estate agents are constantly trying to create mini bubbles in areas. This is good for business: it creates more jobs, more bonuses, more promotions and more opportunities. During the downturn in the property market, estate agents were closing at an alarming rate and people were getting laid off all the time. These mini bubbles also temporarily help the local economy of an area as new services open and existing ones put their prices up. Fancy restaurants move in, pubs are refurbished and – if the bubble really takes hold – infrastructure improves. Parks and pedestrian areas are created, and roads are resurfaced. Sometimes, if the bubble looks really strong, new transport links are planned.

The important point to note here is that when a buy-to-let investor puts in a below-asking-price offer on a property, they are putting in an offer on an already inflated price. When they get their offer accepted, they think they have a bargain. However, all they've got is a discount on an inflated price. The chances are they are paying the market price or even slightly more. Why do people do that? Because they are driven by fear. When they find a good property that ticks all the right boxes, they believe they will never find a better one. And this is the problem with sourcing properties through estate agents.

> **When you find a property through an estate agent, you will rarely get a deal. If you want to *sell* your property quickly or if you want to make a paper profit when you *buy*, you will never do either through an estate agent.**

If you are completely new to the market, without a home to release equity from, your problem is the same as any first-time buyer. You have to save up for a deposit. And we've already shown that to be virtually impossible on an average salary. If the price of the property you want to buy is £200,000, you will need £50,000 (25% for a buy-to-let loan; even more than you need for somewhere that is your primary residence). Even if you can save £300 a month, it would take you 167 months (almost 14 years). And do you think that the property you wanted is still £200,000 at that point? The answer is … no!

First-time buyers can sometimes get a loan with a 10% deposit for a primary residence, but they will generally get a terrible interest rate on this.

So, here's the bottom line. Unless you have inherited money or you are sitting on some equity in your existing home, or you've been given money by your family, you have very little chance of starting your portfolio as a property investor *via the old deal*. If you want get started as a property investor these days, I believe your only option is to learn how to do it using the **new deal**.

5

Understanding The New Deal

So if the "old deal" does not work, how do you become a property investor at all? Well, as you now know ... being a successful property investor in today's market is all about *controlling* property rather than *owning* property. Later in the book we'll look at the different strategies that will help you to *control* property, but first let's look make sure we really understand that the heart of the "new deal" is to frame our involvement in the property market as a *business*.

Principally, let's not forget that our core objective here is to make money; we are just using property as a vehicle for making money like any other investment strategy. Thus, from this point on, let's not think of ourselves as "property investors", let's stick to my preferred term, **PROPERTY ENTREPRENEUR** and get to grips with what it takes to build and run a successful **PROPERTY BUSINESS**.

Positioning

Any businessperson will tell you that the most important factor in becoming successful in your business is how you **position** yourself. If you want to be a property entrepreneur, you need to position yourself to sellers as someone who can help them sell their property quickly and hassle-free; you want to *position* yourself as someone who can give sellers benefits that the high-street estate agent can't.

Think of the property world in these terms: a) there are currently, and at any given time, millions of people around the world who want to sell their homes quickly but don't know how; and b) there are millions of people with money to invest in property who don't have the time to source deals. You need to put yourself in the *position* of helping both these groups of people … while helping yourself at the same time!

Traditionally, when people want to sell their properties, they go to estate agents. They are conditioned to believe this is the only way to sell their property. For many years, estate agents have had the monopoly on selling houses. But an estate agent's motive is always to get as much money as possible (to line their pockets with, because they are working on a commission). If you are a property owner and *your* motive is to sell as quickly as possible, then your motive and the estate agent's motive are in conflict.

When estate agents put properties on the market, they always inflate the price. This is largely what drives the property market up. Estate agents play a kind of "sit and wait" game. They put the property on the market and then they wait to see if they get any interest. They chance their luck by putting it on as high as they dare. If there are few viewings and no serious interest, it means that the price is too high. So they bring the price down a little bit and then wait. They will keep doing this. Weeks and months could go by before they get an offer. Eventually the property will be sold at a price, but the agent will never put the property on offer at that price because they are trying to get as much commission as possible.

The estate agent does not have the seller's interests at heart *nor* the buyer's interests at heart, they are exclusively thinking of their own pockets, no matter what they say! Their motivation is simply to make as much money as possible.

Most sellers don't understand that they are pawns in the estate agent's profit-making game. Some sellers are selling because they *want* to make as much money as possible. In which case they are best placed with an estate agent … their motives are in line. But for sellers who need to prioritize speed and an assured sale over profit, an estate agent can be the worst place they can go to sell their house.

As we've said before, there can be many reasons why a seller needs an urgent and assured sale. Remember, not every motivated seller is in a desperate financial situation. Sellers may be motivated because they want to release their equity for a divorce settlement; it could be because they have to relocate for work; it could be because they've inherited a mortgaged property and don't want the responsibility of renting it out – they'd rather get as much equity out as they can as quickly as possible and move on.

Having said all this, it is the ones who *are* facing repossession who most urgently need the help of cash-rich investors. The whole economic miracle that started in the late 90s was fuelled by debt under the so-called "New Labour" government. Our "growth" was actually financed with credit cards, loans and huge mortgages that were secured on bad debts themselves. As a result, since the crash, countless people are on debt repayment plans and IVAs. Some people have reached the place where they just want to get rid of their mortgage and be free of some of their debt. If you have been made redundant and cannot make your mortgage payments, and you have little or no (or worse, *negative*) equity in your property, then you need a solution *fast!* The longer it takes to release yourself from the commitment of mortgage repayments, the further into arrears you sink. You run the risk of spiralling further and further into debt as the lender prepares a repossession order. You could move out quickly and rent your property, but this can take time because you need to ask your lender's permission, get your house ready for renters, advertise and get people in, etc., and time is not on your side! If you are in this position, you cannot afford to list your house with an estate agent and wait for them to play their profit-making games!

This is where the *positioning* for a property entrepreneur comes in. You have the *opportunity* to put yourself in the position to be able to help people who need to sell their property quickly and for whom the estate agent is not going to be of much use.

You do not have to wait for the next economic crash to get into this position. People get into difficulty in all market conditions. When the market is buoyant, they over-leverage their property (borrow too much against the inflated value of the property, leaving them exposed to getting into negative equity when the market dips again), and when the market is weak and the economy is struggling, people lose their jobs, lose confidence and end up not being able to pay their mortgage.

Property entrepreneurs position themselves to be able to make money in all market conditions.

Think In Terms Of Terms!

I'm constantly hearing property investors talking only about *price*. They boast about how they've negotiated a fantastic deal, but it's always the price. One will say, "I got a 30% BMV deal", and the next investor will say, "Great. But I just got a 40% BMV deal."

In this new era of property investing, if you want to be a successful property entrepreneur you *must* learn to negotiate great **terms** as well as a good price. **It is the TERMS of the deal that will determine your control over the property.** And remember … it's all about *control*.

To negotiate the best terms, you *must* deal directly with the seller. You cannot negotiate the best deal for both you and the seller if there's a middleman (such as an estate agent or auctioneer) in the way.

Remember: you are a negotiator, which means you need to understand give and take. You can't go to a seller and demand everything you want with no consideration for their situation. You must work with them. **Remember your position as a *solution provider*.** You are looking to get the best possible solution based on their circumstances. As such, you must start to see the property business as a **people business**. You need to listen to people in the way that a doctor or a dentist would listen to people. You are a **consultant** trying to find the best **plan** for the seller, one that also satisfies what you want as an investor.

The New Dealmaker

In the past, if someone said they were a property investor, they usually meant that they invested in property on the side. Most people had a job or ran a business and invested in property "on the side" as a way of ensuring a nest egg for the future and providing an additional income. There was a time when everyone you spoke to seemed to do a little investing in property. This was because, for a stretch of time (loosely about 20 years from about the mid 80s until the big crash of 2008/9), the ease of getting financing for property made it possible for almost anyone to become a property investor. However, since the crash, with lenders making it increasingly difficult to secure financing – and especially as the market has recovered and the rise in property prices has made it so difficult for first-time buyers to get on the property ladder – would-be investors have had to think more creatively about how they operate.

In the current financial climate, if you are really serious about making property the foundation of your asset-based wealth, you *have* to treat it as a business and think creatively about it. You can't just buy a couple of houses with buy-to-let mortgages and then rent them out. Ideally you need a portfolio of 10 or more properties that you control, sometimes in unconventional ways. It is still possible to invest in property on an *ad hoc* basis, but the smart investor now knows that you have to approach the property game as a really serious enterprise. Thus you need to possess – or develop – the kinds of skills that are associated with starting up any business. You have to become entrepreneurial, which is why I refer to someone building up a property business in this way as a property entrepreneur.

Entrepreneurial Qualities

So what is an entrepreneur? An entrepreneur is someone who is creative, who develops ideas and nurtures them to fruition. Entrepreneurs are not bound by rules; and they can be contrarians. If the crowd is going one way, entrepreneurs will go in the opposite direction. They follow a different paradigm; they will make the impossible possible. If you tell an entrepreneur that something can't be done, their immediate response will be "well let's find a way in which it *can* be done". Entrepreneurs are usually good leaders; they build good teams and know how to utilize resources, they have a way of analysing their resources, working out what they lack and then acquiring what they need. They keep pushing forward towards their goals. They are resourceful; they are strategists who think outside of the box. They work harder than most people and make sacrifices along the way.

Entrepreneurs are **problem solvers**; they are experts in finding solutions. **A property entrepreneur's "problem solving" skills are almost more important than his or her monetary resources.** Remember: whatever you lack in monetary resources, you can make up for in skills and creativity. In fact, you never really do lack resources because you *always* have your skills and creativity at your disposal. In the long term, your skills and creativity are *more* valuable than your monetary resources. Once you've spent your money, it's gone; but if you are creative and have entrepreneurial skills, you will always be able to use them to find and raise monetary resources.

We love watching entrepreneurs in action. That's why shows like *The Apprentice* are so popular. We love to watch people bravely take risks that we might not be prepared to take. Entrepreneurs take massive risks. They understand the concept of taking risks *now* in order to protect their future. They see a life without risk as being a greater risk in the long term because if you reach old age without having built your security and stability, you will be dependent on someone else – the state, or your family perhaps – and that's a more frightening prospect to an entrepreneur than the fear they may feel about taking risk now. Entrepreneurs are always prepared to give up time and freedom now because they know they are creating a foundation to get unlimited time and freedom in the future. They believe in and are focused on the end results.

But the main difference between an entrepreneur and someone in a job is that an entrepreneur gets paid based purely on their own results. The risk is that they may put in a huge amount of work and get nothing out; but the other side of the coin is that they may actually get astronomical results ... and the best thing is, they get to keep them! You might get a secure income in a salaried job, but you'll never get the full reward for your efforts ... most of that will always go to your employer.

Most people would not be prepared to do what an entrepreneur would be prepared to do. Many people call themselves entrepreneurs without a clue of what it really takes to be one. They fail at their businesses and they don't know why, so they give up and go back to the well-travelled path of salaried security. Most people want to follow a safe routine: they get up, they go to work, they get their monthly pay cheque, they come home and order a pizza, and then they sit on the sofa and watch TV. They live robotically, effectively switching off their brains so that they don't have to deal with anything that frightens them or makes them feel uncomfortable. What these people don't realize is that they are taking the biggest risk of all, because if they were suddenly to lose their jobs, they would have virtually nothing. Even if they think they are secure because they have some savings in the bank or because they "own" their own home, they are deluding themselves, because if their salary suddenly stopped and they were unable to get a new job (increasingly likely as they get older), those savings would be quickly wiped out and, if they were unable to pay their monthly mortgage, their house would be repossessed.

An entrepreneur doesn't understand this mindset. To an entrepreneur you are *not* "safe", you are *not* secure, until you have financial freedom. **Financial freedom is the knowledge that you will always be able to finance your life, through your assets and passive income**.

Entrepreneurs do not make excuses for their procrastination. If they don't have capital, they go out and raise it; if they don't have knowledge, they will go out and acquire it. In fact, one of the biggest myths about entrepreneurs – a huge misconception people have – is the notion that successful entrepreneurs all had a big capital base to build from. This is rarely the case. In fact, young people who start off with a lot of money tend not to do as well as those who start out with nothing but who have the essential passionate entrepreneurial spirit.

Successful entrepreneurs rarely use their own money (i.e. cash they've earned and paid tax on) to start an enterprise, even when they do become wealthy.

The problem is, entrepreneurs make it look too easy. They are like swans, gliding along the surface, hardly making a ripple on it, while underneath their legs are paddling like mad! Others try to copy them and fail, because they don't realize how much hard work really goes on behind closed doors!

Another trait of successful entrepreneurs is that they find and surround themselves with people who are doing better than them, not with people who are always failing. A lot of people do the opposite; they surround themselves with people who are slightly less well-off and successful than them in order to make themselves feel better – it feeds their egos. But this will never give them inspiration; they will never learn strategies from people who are failing. You only learn how to improve your own skills by watching people who are *more* successful than you. The most successful entrepreneurs always surround themselves with people who are more successful than them, people who will inspire them to reach for a higher bar.

Of course, there are successful entrepreneurs and less successful entrepreneurs. The whole point, though, is to keep striving for solutions. Ultimately, that is what entrepreneurs do: they find problems and solve them. They are constantly growing and evolving, using their learning experiences as building blocks. The point of being an entrepreneur is not to have everything rosy, but to have the ability to deal with whatever problems occur. An entrepreneur *expects* problems and challenges.

Bruce Lee said: **"Do not pray for an easy life, pray for the strength to endure a difficult one."**

A Winning Perspective

For the most part in life, your attitude is everything. If you have the right mindset, you will succeed. The worst attitude you can have is one where you point the finger at others and blame them for your circumstances. So many people do this. They blame their parents, or a partner or a sibling for why they haven't been successful in life. But ultimately no one is to blame for where you are but *you*, because you always have the ability to change your attitude and start achieving whatever you strive for. An entrepreneur always takes responsibility for what goes on around him or her. If you lose money in the stock market, it's *your* decision. If you fail, it's because of the choices *you* took. But an entrepreneur doesn't sit around bemoaning these misfortunes; an entrepreneur gets up and learns from their mistakes and starts afresh.

One of my favourite stories – that John Lee and I told in *The Wealth Dragon Way* – is the story of the twin brothers who were fostered. Here's a quick précis of the story.

Their father was an alcoholic and their mother abandoned them. They were both fostered into different families. One eventually became an incredibly successful businessman and the other became an unemployed drifter with a drug problem. A journalist interviewed them for an article he was writing. He asked the unsuccessful brother, the one with a drug problem, how he had sunk so low and got into this situation. He said, "With parents like mine, what would you expect?" The journalist then went to interview the other brother about how he had become so successful. He said, "With parents like mine, what would you expect?"

If you want to be a successful entrepreneur, you *must* get the right attitude. You can't repeat old, unproductive mantras like, "I've been told this can't be done …" or "I can't do that because …". You have to say, "I've been told this can't be done but I think I've found a way to do it", or "I don't think I can do that but I'm willing to give it a try".

At the end of the day, you should do **whatever it takes** (within legal and ethical bounds) to get where you want to be.

Having said this, contrary to what many people believe, **legality** is not black and white. Any lawyer will tell you this. Obviously there are laws, but these can be interpreted. There will always be debate; there is always grey area. That's the reason we have lawyers, to debate the interpretation of the law. If you hire a lawyer, his or her job is to know how to interpret the law to your advantage. Where one lawyer will say you *can't*, another lawyer will find a way in which you *can* that is technically legal. If there is a way in which you can push something through, you should … as long as it doesn't infringe on someone else's rights.

At a seminar I was giving in Malaysia recently, the audience began asking me if acquiring property using lease-option deals was legal. They were concerned because they weren't aware of such deals being done in the past before I mentioned I'd done some. I explained that my forward-thinking lawyer had done adequate research to prove that it was not *il*legal. Entrepreneurs should be the ones writing the new rulebooks!

You should apply the same rule to ethics. Ask yourself if something feels *unethical* and if it does, don't do it. If it doesn't feel unethical, then you can consider it ethical, even if it hasn't been done before.

Everyone has an ethical code they are comfortable with. I am comfortable with my ethical code. Some people feel that buying houses below the market value is unethical. I feel it's more unethical to leave someone in a house that they are about to be evicted from and have the bank repossess when there is something you could have done (for a price, of course, you are not a charity). I run a business, I am philanthropic in other ways – I give a lot of money to charity and local causes – but when it comes to property deals, I have to make a profit.

In any case, "market value" is an arbitrary thing. Something is only worth what someone will pay for it. If someone has been unable to sell their house at the "market value" and they urgently need to sell, then they need to reconsider the supposed "value" of their house (the value to *them*!). When I create a win-win situation, I believe I give the seller great value because I help them move on with their lives. In any case, they always have a choice. When I make a BMV offer, they have the choice to say no. But I will still only offer what gives me the best deal. If someone has a house worth £200,000, I will offer them around £160,000. If they say no, that's fine (although this probably means that the sale is not as urgent as they said it was). Remember, not everyone is looking for a quick sale because they are about to be repossessed. Some people simply want to release the equity urgently and don't want to go through an estate agent who will be obsessed with money and potentially take months to sell the house.

Imagine an elderly couple who, on retirement, have decided they want to emigrate to Australia to be with their son's family. They have a house worth £200,000 that they bought 30 years ago and have paid off the mortgage on. They can sell to me for £160,000 and be in Australia within a matter of weeks. Or they can hold on and wait for a sale that might not come for a year or so. Why wouldn't they take up my offer? Every day on the beach with their grandchildren is precious. Isn't an extra £40,000, which might not even materialize because the market could drop before they get their perceived "full market value", a price worth paying in order to be able to start their new life immediately? Can you imagine the difference between knowing you have a guaranteed sale and being able to book your flights and organize your life, versus sitting around doing nothing, waiting while the estate agent trickles a slow stream of viewers through your door for a year? You can't really put a price on freedom. If I offer them a guaranteed sale and a date by which the sale will go through, I give them the freedom to start their new lives. In my opinion that is highly ethical!

Many sellers approach me because they simply don't want to deal with estate agents. Some of them have had bad experiences in the past and can't afford to lose any more time. If someone has a lot of equity in their house and they want it released urgently, I am offering them a great opportunity. They might have bought the house for £50,000 15 years ago and only have a £20,000 mortgage on it. The estate agents might say it's worth £200,000, but how do they know if and when they will get that figure? If I offer £160,000, they are still getting £140,000 out of it. As the old proverb goes ... a bird in the hand is worth two in the bush!

On the flip side, if someone has got into mortgage arrears and is being threatened with repossession, they probably have no equity left in the house because they have probably already remortgaged to cover past mortgage payments. These people can't afford to wait around for an estate agent to get them the full market value; they need a way out immediately. If a seller doesn't have any equity in the property, I can help them move on with their lives (as you will soon see when I explain how I do a lease-option deal). I can make money and I can help *them* make money in the long run.

Later in the book, I will be showing you many different strategies that will enable you to structure your deals so that they work best for you and for the seller, but the important thing at this stage is to grasp the overall notion that the "new deal" is all about learning to treat property as a business and, thus, yourself as an entrepreneurial business owner.

Before we look at those specific strategies, in the next two chapters we will look at some of the fundamental principles and systems that I believe are essential to building a successful property business.

CHAPTER 6

Starting Your Property Business

Whether or not you *feel* like a businessperson, if you want to become a property entrepreneur, you are going to have to *become* a businessperson. You are going to be doing business with all kinds of people, in many different ways, so you must start to *think* like a businessperson and *look* like a business person.

The first thing I ask people when they come to me saying that they want to become property investors, is: how many cash-rich investors do you know? Most of the time, they tell me that they don't know any. Well, if you don't know any cash-rich investors, to whom are you going to flip a deal when you find one? So you have to work backwards. You have to create demand first. Find cash-rich investors who are looking for deals, build a relationship with them and *then* go out and find a deal. How do you find investors? You need to start getting involved and being seen in the business. Go to conferences, read up as much as you can, go to networking events. Get into "the scene"! Ideally, you want to be in touch with at least 50 cash-rich investors before you go and source deals.

You might baulk at this idea, because if you've never known a cash-rich investor you might not really believe they exist. Well, of course they exist! They are everywhere. And they are looking for deals. Who are they? They are the successful business owners all around you. They are the car rental business owners, the restaurateurs, the beauty salon owners, the delivery company owners; they want to find places to invest their money but they are busy running their businesses – they don't have time to be property entrepreneurs as well. They are looking for savvy property entrepreneurs to bring the deals *to them*.

At this point you are probably still wondering where these investors are and how on earth you find them. Believe me, once you become aware that they are around, they will pop up everywhere!

As with anything in life, you only notice what is around you once you become consciously aware of something. For instance, I wasn't aware of having seen many Aston Martins in my time. Then I bought my Aston Martin and suddenly I saw them everywhere. Every day, I'd see one. They were there before but they just weren't registering on my radar. Trust me, once you start looking for cash-rich investors, once you really put yourself out there and let people *know* you are looking for cash-rich investors, you will start coming across them everywhere.

Most people are shy about getting into property. They don't believe that there are people out there with money ready to invest in property. But there is an endless supply of existing and upcoming cash-rich investors looking for a place to put their money from where they can earn a reasonable return. You have to go out and look for them; they are unlikely simply to pop up in your life arbitrarily. You must start talking to people about your intention to get into the property business. You have to start building your business, and part of that is networking. Once you start telling people about your new enterprise and how you are sourcing property deals, you will quickly come across investors who will be willing to go into JVs (joint ventures) with you.

Beware, however, if you are going for a mortgage using money from a JV as the deposit. Lenders don't generally like this and will try to penalize you. They want to see that the deposit is all your own money, coming from your own savings, which we've already established is near impossible. However, there are various ways you can get around the lenders' objections. It is always best to buy the property outright and then take out a mortgage (if possible) once you own the property.

What you *don't* want to do is to go out and find your deals first and *then* look for investors. How can you offer a seller a guaranteed deal without cash-rich investors in place?

In effect, cash-rich investors take the place of your traditional deposit and mortgage structure.

You need to get over the potential awkwardness that most people feel when they ask for money. Remember, you are not asking for a gift! You are giving investors an opportunity. You are offering them a great return on their investment without having to do much work. The deal is *you* are doing the lion's share of the work for the opportunity to use their money. They are getting a well-researched, high-return investment opportunity while hardly having to lift a finger. It's win-win!

Create Demand First

So many people going into business fail to grasp the concept of creating demand first and waste a lot of their time and money. Have you ever seen those "bargain buckets" near the cash registers in shops? They are filled with items that haven't sold. Mostly this is because someone has created a product before creating demand. People who have gone away and thought, "I know what would be a really cool product and I'm going to go and make it", without figuring out if anyone will ever actually buy it! These items all end up in that bargain bucket being sold for a fraction of their original retail price. The creators of these products believed they were making life-changing products, but half the time they were just legends in their own minds. They hadn't created the demand so they had no idea if anyone would actually buy the precious goods they'd spent hours and hours making.

It's amazing how many people do this. They create a product first and then they take it to market. This is the wrong way round. You want to create demand first and ensure that there *is* a market for your product before you start to sell it. Remember 'Del Boy' Trotter in *Only Fools and Horses*? His council flat was always full to bursting with boxes and boxes of rubbish; products that he was convinced people would want to buy, but ended up being unable to *give* away. That's not how you want to end up!

So find out what your market (your potential JV partners) really wants. Most investors are simply looking for a return on investment, so show them exactly that. If you show this level of expertise, perhaps your JV partners will even provide you with a marketing budget, up front, to source the kind of deals they want.

Would YOU Invest In You?

Before you approach anyone about doing a JV, before you ask anyone to invest in you, you need to ask yourself one serious question. Would *you* invest in you? In order to answer this, you need to take a good hard look at everything about you, from the way you dress to the way you speak. I don't mean your accent, I mean the language you use.

I remember a woman in a property seminar I was giving, standing up and saying: "Vince, you've got loads of money, can you lend me some money so that I can start a business." The audience was aghast at her audacity. I never mind being asked for money, but if this woman really wanted me to invest in her, she was going about it in completely the wrong way. I just looked at her and smiled. I asked her:

"Are you a businessperson or a beggar? Because right now, you sound like you are begging for money from me. Entrepreneurs don't go around begging for money, they offer business proposals. So what is your proposal? What's in it for me?"

Of course this woman didn't have a proposal worked out. She had wasted an opportunity. That's not to say I wouldn't have looked at a proposal had she brought me one a few days later (which, of course, she didn't), but the first impression she had made had not been a good one and she would need to work extra hard to bring me around the next time.

Don't get into this situation. Get all your ducks in a row, do all your research, present an attractive package. Show them what's in it for them. *Asking* for money from someone you don't know is basically asking for charity. Many wealthy people already give a huge amount to worthy causes every year. Why would they give charity to you? *Offering* an opportunity is a totally different ball game. You are telling them what is in it for them; you are making it an attractive offer. If that woman had stood up and said: "You know Vince, you seem like a really savvy entrepreneur who is always looking for good investment opportunities. I have a fantastic opportunity that is really too good to miss. I think you'll be very excited when you hear about it. Would you like to meet in the coffee break for a few minutes so I can tell you about it?" She might have got a better response from me!

Take a really good look at yourself in the mirror. Do you *look* like a businessperson? Or do you look like you did when you were rocking up to student lectures five or ten years ago? If someone is considering doing business with you, and it's a toss-up between you and another person who looks more presentable, who do you think will win? The way you present yourself could be the determining factor. Of course you might have a great pitch, but so might the other – more presentable – person. In the end, if the pitches are more or less the same and they have to choose on one factor, it might well be on which candidate presented themselves the best. So always make sure you present yourself well. It sounds so obvious, but I can't believe how many times I've seen people fall down on appearance, even when they have a really viable investment opportunity. So be clean! Wear clean, smart clothes; don't wear jeans. Go reasonably conservative; don't wear some outlandish fashion item. Comb your hair. Make sure your hands and nails are clean!

The importance of **punctuality** obviously goes without saying. If I ask someone to meet me at my office at 9am and they saunter in at 10.15am without an apology or explanation, I'm not going to do business with them.

You should also invest a great deal of time in your pitch. It should be sound and confident. You *must* know all your figures. How many times have you seen, on *Dragons' Den*, a really good pitch fall apart when the person is questioned about the figures? There's no excuse … know your figures! In fact, you should watch *Dragons' Den* if you don't already. You will pick up lots of great tips from it. You need a vision. If you can't sum up your vision in two sentences, you don't have one.

I also believe that our **integrity** is everything. Talk is cheap. So many people talk a good talk. But not so many walk the walk. It's what you actually *do*, not what you *say*, that counts in the end. Be true to your word; make sure your actions reflect exactly what you've promised.

Don't forget that all the little things add up to an overall impression. If you look clean, you turn up on time, your business card looks stylish and professional, you always answer emails promptly and professionally, and you deliver whatever you've promised – you stand the best chance.

You also need to show what experience you have. You must have *some* experience. If you don't have any yet, go and get some!

Having said all of this, for me, the most important factor when I'm considering doing business with someone is **likeability**.

If I don't like you, I don't want to do business with you, no matter how good your figures are or how presentable you look. If I *do* like you, I will forgive the odd mistake on the balance sheet (that's something I can easily correct) or the coffee stain on your sleeve.

People do business with people they like. That is the bottom line.

How likeable are you? Ask people how you come across. Have a good, honest look at yourself. Do you come across as arrogant?

Do you talk too much? Do you have any little irritating habits? Get ruthless and make some changes if you want to do well in the property business.

Again, I really cannot stress strongly enough why I feel it is essential to treat property investing like a *business*. Property investing is no longer for the casual investor; you have to treat it like a serious business. You really have to pound the pavements and do your work. There are incredible rewards at the end of the day, but they don't come easy.

I really do believe that, unless you have a chunk of money to play with, you can't invest in property as a hobby anymore, the way people used to do; the rules have changed, making investing in property more and more difficult. You *must* have an entrepreneurial mindset to deal with the problems of property investing in today's economic climate. If you keep trying the traditional way, going to lenders to try and get a mortgage, you might eventually get somewhere, but the likelihood is that you'll be spinning your wheels. You'll probably go two steps forward and two steps back and bang your head against a lot of walls, getting increasingly frustrated. So why not find an easier way to do it? Think outside of the box; think like an entrepreneur and look at property investing through a different lens, as a business.

I'm not trying to sell this idea to you. If you don't have a burning desire to do this, don't do it; property is no longer something you can afford to dabble in; you have to be absolutely serious about it. It's a fantastic opportunity but you have to be prepared to do the work.

CHAPTER

A Systemized Business Is A Successful Business

The most successful businesses are systemized, but many businesses are not systemized. If a business is not systemized, business owners spend all their time running the business. When you systemize and strategize your business, it runs itself and grows itself. You put the people and systems in place to do everything for you. Then (if you want, as most entrepreneurs do), you can go off and start another business.

What is a system? A system is a machine that you work very hard to set up, but once it is set up, it works automatically. Or as my business partner puts it … "autoMAGICally"!

To demonstrate the value of a system, when I'm teaching I always use the following story.

There was once a village that was experiencing a drought, so the chief ordered the villagers to build and fill a reservoir with water. They dig the reservoir and then set about trying to fill it with water taken from a river a mile away. To make things more interesting, the villagers decided to have a competition to see who could carry the most water buckets from the river to the reservoir. One particular guy disappeared from the group and was not seen again for months. Everyone else assumed that they were ahead in the game and that this guy would lose. However, one day, about three months later, he turns up and shows them all a tap he has constructed on the edge of the reservoir – that is at the end of a pipeline he'd connected to the river. He turns on the tap and water flows in, filling the reservoir. He obviously won the competition by a landslide!

This guy had figured out how to build the most efficient system. Even though it looked as if he'd done nothing for three months (i.e. he hadn't been putting any water into the reservoir), he'd had a plan. He'd built a system that had more than fulfilled all his needs.

This story is a great metaphor, showing how building a system can take a long time and require a lot of hard work. For ages you might see no results and it might look like you're never going to succeed. But one day, you "turn on the tap" and the results come flooding out. This is exactly what happened to Alan Turing when he was building his Turing Machine. For a long time it did nothing, and then suddenly it started churning out the results that helped Britain win the war and laid the groundwork for modern day computer technology.

Any successful business owner knows that a profitable business is also a system. **The best way to maximize your profits is to systemize your business.** You build a machine – which might take you a long time – but when you push the start button, the results come out.

There are three important components that together constitute a good property business – that indeed are essential to any successful business. These are:

1. A marketing system.

2. A sales system.

3. Dealmaking strategies.

And what you get as a result of these three aspects working well together within one system is *value*. So I call these components together … a well-balanced value system (Figure 7.1).

In this chapter we will look specifically at the first two parts of the model, namely the marketing system and sales system. Marketing and sales techniques are fairly standard and applicable to any business. What makes every business unique is what you literally "feed" into the machine. In this case it will be the actual property deals you make using your specific dealmaking strategies. My tried and tested dealmaking strategies are the heart of this book and we will be covering them in the next chapter.

Let's look closely at how to build the marketing and sales systems that will contribute to the success of your property business.

Figure 7.1   A Well-Balanced Value System

The Marketing System

A successful property business depends on getting *motivated sellers* into the system. So let's start with **marketing**. How do you market to get motivated sellers?

Well, firstly, what *is* marketing? Marketing is targeting a specific audience for your business. It's about getting your message out to the right people. You reach out to the people who you believe would like to buy your product or services. If you are a property entrepreneur, the message you want to put out there is that you are in a position to help people quickly relieve themselves of the responsibility of their property and move on with their lives.

Marketing is all about **positioning**. To get your position right, you need to understand the 5 Ps of marketing: **Products**, **Place**, **Promotion**, **Price** and **Profit**.

Products

What is it that you are actually offering to people? A product can be a physical product or a service. As a property entrepreneur, you are offering a service through which you help people offload their properties quickly. You need to describe what your service is and how it is a different experience from going to an estate agent. In my business, I am also looking to recruit motivated *buyers* because

I don't necessarily want to take on every property I do a deal on – some of them I want to flip. So I am marketing two services: **helping people sell their homes fast** and **finding deals for investors**.

Here's a very important point about the second part of your service (finding investors). If you want to start up as a property investor and you don't have any of your own money, or at least not enough to buy houses, you can still build a highly-successful business. Remember, there are people out there who *do* have money. If you can find investors who have liquid resources, and you have leads to sellers who need to sell up fast, you can make deals. When I approach a seller with a deal, I am representing a group of investors with ready cash. This puts me in the same position as an individual cash buyer. When I started my business I called it **NETWORK PROPERTY BUYERS** for this very reason! Now, of course, I have my own cash to invest, but when I started out, I didn't. I represented cash-rich buyers, which gave me enormous negotiating power. Yes, I guess I have been that middleman! But I still think I operate more ethically than most estate agents.

Place

When I say "place" I really mean **positioning**. We have to position ourselves for a specific market; we can't be all things to all people. We need to segment the market, to take a specific segment and become an expert in it. The people in this particular segment are your consumers – the people who will consume your particular product or use your particular service. You need to know what the consumers in your segment want. We are not positioning ourselves to appeal to people who want to buy or sell multi-million pound high-end properties here. We are going to be dealing with ordinary people who need to sell their house quickly.

The common perception of a property investor is someone who deals with extraordinary properties, but if you're becoming the type of investor I'm talking about here – a property entrepreneur – you will be dealing with very ordinary properties. It's not a particularly glamorous segment of the market, but it's a profitable one and one that is available to everyone. You don't need to have extraordinary skills either, you just need to be able to talk to ordinary people and be able to learn some specific techniques. This type of property investing is about doing common property transactions with common people; we're dealing with Joe Blogs, we're not selling to the Sultan of Brunei or the Beckhams! Furthermore, we are dealing with Joe Blogs who is in a *particular* situation, who needs to sell his property quickly. He needs help. So that is how you have to position yourself, as someone who can *help*.

Place is also about distinguishing yourself from others. In particular you need to distinguish yourself from the estate agents. You need to tell people why you are a better option than an estate agent in this particular situation. Your market is like a huge pond, you have to know which fish you want and sit where they are likely to swim and dangle the bait that they prefer to eat. Take heart ... our section of the pond (the market) is very large, in fact even bigger than the multi-million pound segment. There are countless ordinary people with ordinary properties and many of them unfortunately get into situations where they need to sell their property quickly. These are the people you need to talk to; this is **your market**.

Remember, for every property for sale there is a seller with a reason for selling. You need to know the range of reasons *your* market has. Your market does not include sellers whose reasons are, "I need to make as much profit as possible" or "I need to make a certain figure so that I can buy my next house but I don't know when I can move because I'm in a chain". The range of reasons *your* market has includes, "I need to sell my house before I accrue any more arrears on my mortgage, which I can't pay because I lost my job" or "I need to sell my late mother's house to release the equity in it to put it towards another property I'm buying and the sale has to go through in less than six weeks". The reason must always include a deadline because that is what you are able to offer: a fast sale in a guaranteed space of time. They need a guaranteed completion date as soon as possible.

Your market is made up of people who need to sell quickly and assuredly.

Promotion

Once you've identified *where* to position yourself to attract your audience, you need to figure out *how* to attract them. How do you get your message out to them? This is all about advertising, which can be **push** or **pull** advertising.

Push advertising is like door-to-door selling. You have to work really hard to get the message out to people. You're always trying to get referrals; in other words, asking people to refer you to anyone they know who is trying to sell their property quickly. You incentivize them by offering to pay them a fee for any deals you get through their referrals. You're continually pushing the message out to your audience. Telesales is an example of push advertising, when you are constantly making phone calls to people, trying to get a sale. You can apply this to your property business. For example, if you identify an empty home that looks as though it has been abandoned and is in serious disrepair, you can call the council to find out who is the owner so that you can offer your services to him or her. The council may or may not release that information, but you should keep trying (perhaps by calling different departments or waiting a while and calling back with the hope that the property has become of greater concern) because the longer the house remains abandoned, the more of a problem it becomes for the council. Abandoned homes are a serious environmental hazard. They attract squatters, rats and vandals. Vandals will break in to steal anything; they will rip copper wires out of the walls and strip the house of anything they can physically move.

There are many reasons why a property might have been abandoned. Perhaps it is owned by a landlord who couldn't afford to complete some repairs after his last tenants left and hasn't been able to re-let it. Of course, on a property that has been left in disrepair or vandalized, there is an element of development to be done, but that is a second potential profit. The primary profit should come from the fact that you are able to get the property for a BMV deal because the owner is so motivated to sell. (Remember the "market value" is always what the property is worth *in its current condition*, not what it *will* be once you've renovated it. Many people misunderstand this.) The owner might have given up on it; he might be unable to sell or rent it and yet is still paying the mortgage because he doesn't want it repossessed. If a property lies empty for too long, the council might get a court order to force the owner to sell. Some councils even buy the properties themselves – at a significant BMV price – to add to their own housing stock. If the property needs too much work, the council may not even want to buy it. If you can get hold of the information about the property at the point at which the council has obtained a court order to force the owner to sell, you're in the ideal position to offer your service to the owner. You can step in and buy at a BMV price. At the end of the day, it's in the council's interest to help you offer your services to the owner because they don't want abandoned properties sitting around attracting problems.

You can also try to procure lists of properties that are going through repossession. You have to be careful though, because the sources of these lists can be a bit dubious. If these lists are being sold, then chances are you are not the only person who has seen them and the seller may already have been hounded by would-be buyers. You may find half the phone numbers have been disconnected. You might find the odd live lead if you try hard enough for long enough, but this whole process forces you to be extremely pushy and you have to question how efficient it is. Some people think they are rather "clever" by employing quite extreme methods; some even go so far as sitting outside courtrooms waiting for people to be charged with a repossession order, like ambulance chasers (no win – no fee accident lawyers who pitch their services to people literally as they are getting out of an ambulance). It's not perhaps the best way to go about advertising your services, but it is an option.

If you find a seller who has just been served with a repossession order, you know exactly how long they have got before the lender takes away the property. You can't change the fact that they are in debt to the lender, but you can explain to the owner that you can guarantee them a sale before the repossession order takes effect – the court usually gives the owner an extension of three to six months to try to sell the property and release any equity in it before they are evicted. Of course, all the mortgage arrears have to be paid off – something that you might have to factor into the deal – but at least you allow the owner to move out of their own accord and walk away with some dignity instead of being repossessed by the lender. In this situation, you would also find yourself dealing directly with the bank, or whoever the lender is, because you will probably be guaranteeing to pay off the owner's arrears with the equity (something that would normally happen before the sale went through). As long as there is a guarantee that the arrears will be paid off and the sale is going through, the bank may stop the order all together.

Pull advertising is all about *attraction*. It's about making people come to you. You advertise through multiple channels to reveal to people what you can offer them and why you are their best option. It's much nicer having people come to you rather than having to chase them. To get pull advertising right, first you need to know exactly where people are going to get their information. This goes back to your *positioning*.

Most people who have a problem (with anything, not just needing to sell a house quickly) go straight to Google and type words into the search box. They will type in words like "SELL MY HOUSE FAST". You need to be coming up in those search results. When I started as a property investor, I found over 100,000 sellers that way. It's harder now, because more people are doing it, but competition can be healthy and not everyone gets it right, so if you are good at it you will keep coming up with results. And although the keywords have now become extremely expensive, there are new avenues for advertising opening up all the time. Facebook has become a huge advertising platform, as has YouTube.

Advertising is all about being creative and knowing what people will respond to, but you should also be aware that trends tend to go around in cycles. For example, when the Internet first got popular around the mid 90s, when we were still using dial-up and modems, the only way to advertise was by using pop-up banners. Then people got sick of them and started to ignore them. The trend switched to Google ads and text ads based on your search terms. But people have been bombarded with these now and have stopped responding to them; they have grown immune to them. Now, almost 20 years since we first used them, people are responsive to pop-up banners again!

The way people get their information also changes. Again, at one point people used to trust all the information they got from the Internet. But, *again*, after experiencing information overload, people have become more wary and will double-, and even triple-, check their information.

These cyclical trends don't just apply online. There was a time when leafleting worked; then people got sick of leaflets and viewed them as a real nuisance, so advertisers stopped using them and went back to running ads in newspapers. Now advertisers are using leafleting again and apparently it's working as it used to; people are starting to respond to leaflets again.

At the end of the day, there are no hard and fast rules, and it's difficult to know exactly which element of your campaign is or isn't working. You have to be flexible. You have to move with the times; you must **test and measure** consistently to see what works. Many people don't. I've had people come up to me and say, "I've tried leaflets and they don't work" and I've explained that it might not be the *leaflets* that are not working – it might be the *message* in the leaflets that isn't working.

I was once getting out of my car – an Aston Martin – and someone stopped me to admire it. He asked me what I did. I said I was a property investor. But that shouldn't have been a measure of how successful I was. It doesn't matter *what* you do, it matters *how* you do it. If I got a stall selling fruit and vegetables, I'd still be working towards being the most successful greengrocer in the market. I'd devise whatever advertising and sales techniques I needed in order to make the biggest profit.

In the end it doesn't really matter what medium you choose to advertise in, it only matters *how* you advertise within it.

I have people coming to me saying they believe they are unsuccessful because they don't have a website. I explain to them, again, that you can be successful or unsuccessful with a website; that it's not about the website, it's about the message. If you get the message perfect and then do a leafleting campaign you could be incredibly successful.

I always urge people to remember the acronym AIDA when it comes to marketing. That stands for **Attention**, **Interest**, **Desire** and **Action**. Your message must do all of these things: grab their attention, keep their interest, make them desire something and inspire them into taking action. Obviously, grabbing someone's attention is the first, most important, step. You are competing with every other advertiser to get it. How can you ensure that someone looks at your message instead of a competitor's? A lot of advertising is very weak when it comes to grabbing attention. Think about what grabs *yours*. When you open the newspaper, what is it about one headline that makes you read that article rather than another? If a headline doesn't grab your attention, you're not going to read the article.

Price

The price you set is an important part of your marketing strategy because it gives people a perception of the quality of your product.

If you went into a camera shop and you didn't know too much about cameras, and then you saw two very similar looking cameras with almost identical features but one was more expensive than the other, you'd naturally assume the more expensive one was better. That's your *assumption*, but you don't know for sure.

Even though, as a property investor, it is the property owner who is technically selling to *you*, you are still the one who is providing the service and therefore the one who sets the price for that service. The seller doesn't pay you up front; your fee is the **discount** you get when you buy the property. So, you might set your price at 30%. You tell the seller that whatever his property is valued at, you will pay 30% below that and this is not negotiable. He might perceive you as being greedy and ruthless, but the point is a) you *need* that discount, that is your fee for buying what is quite possibly a hard to sell property in a guaranteed length of time, and b) you are not pointing a gun to anyone's head; the seller can walk away if he wants to. Set your price and stick to it!

You don't want the seller to think of you as unreasonable or unfair, but you do need to set your price for your service – which happens to come in the form of a purchase price at a discount on the market value of the property. Maybe 30% sounds like too much, but as an investor you must set your price at whatever you know will make you a profit. You must have a minimum price that you don't go below. For the most part you should keep your price set for all your deals, but some properties will have exceptional circumstances. Depending on the property and what work needs doing to it, you might be able to set your price at 20%, maybe even 10% will allow you to make a profit. The point is, once you've set a price for a particular property, you must not deviate from it, because you have to protect your interests. If you negotiate, you will lose money. The offer you make must be set in stone. This should be one of your golden rules: **never deviate from the price (percentage BMV) that you set**.

If the seller expresses any negativity, you have to remind them, sometimes several times, that they are not *forced* to sell to you. You are offering them what no one else is offering them. The price they are paying (i.e. the discount they are giving you) is the price they need to pay for a guaranteed sale in a short space of time. You have to keep reminding them what they are getting. They are getting peace of mind; they are getting rid of the responsibility of the property that they don't want anymore. They are getting the freedom to move on with their lives. When people tell me something is too expensive, I ask them to think of the alternative. In this scenario, the alternative is prolonging the pain of being in debt and potentially facing eviction. At the end of the day (and I cannot stress this too much), the property owner *always* has a choice. They are not being forced into anything; they are not being exploited, they are being helped.

Of course, price is not the only thing on the negotiating table. As a property entrepreneur, with these new strategies for doing deals, you will **negotiate the terms as well as the price**. Your price is not flexible, but your terms *are*. You may be able to offer something in the *terms* that sweetens the deal. You choose the level of discount that you are happy with, that you can make a profit at, and then there is no room for negotiation – all you have left to negotiate are the **terms**. For example, if a seller has little or no equity in the property, or is even in negative equity, how can you help them when they don't even have any equity in the property to give you a discount on? In this case, you would normally explain how a lease-option deal could work for everyone, and how you would get your discount in the long term. This is a particularly popular strategy for my associates in the Netherlands at the moment, because around a million people there were in negative equity at the beginning of 2015 as property prices had dropped so much in the preceding decade.

Profit

At the end of the day, as I've said before, it's got to be a win-win situation for everyone. It's not just about you profiting, it's about both parties getting what they need from the deal. You get your profit; the seller's "profit" is often simply peace of mind. I believe in adding value to people's lives and getting paid for it, and justifiably so. I've met people who have a problem asking for the profit they deserve because they simply don't believe in themselves. They are too embarrassed to ask for what is due to them. They don't understand the value they bring to other people's lives. If you don't believe in yourself, you'll never get anywhere. You can't be a successful entrepreneur if you don't have the right self-concept.

The gratitude people show me can be overwhelming sometimes. I've had people hug me and break down in tears when I've relieved them of the burden of their property, when I have released them from something that has become toxic to them.

I always remember this woman in the Netherlands whose fiancé had to go back to Turkey. She wanted to go with him immediately, to start their new life together, but she had to stay on in the Netherlands because she couldn't sell her property and she had to keep paying the mortgage. (In the Netherlands it is very difficult to get permission to rent your property out because renters have such powerful rights.) She was being driven mad by postponing the start of her new life and not knowing when she could join her loved one. She couldn't wait to get rid of the property and move to Turkey to be with him. She was so grateful when I did a deal with her and bought the property (I tell this story in more detail in the final part of the book).

Remember, most people are not entrepreneurial types who can think of solutions. They may not have the resources to fix their problems. They *need* help. And you can provide them with that.

We regularly get tokens of appreciation. We get flowers, chocolates and champagne from people who are celebrating the fact that we've helped them move on with their lives. Money isn't everything to everyone. Property investing is my business, so I need to make money on every deal, but for most of the people I deal with, getting rid of their property is far more important than money. Profit is not just monetary; it is any benefit to your life.

The Sales System

Selling is not marketing. Marketing is about *finding* your customers and getting your message across to them; selling is about starting the negotiation process. When you find someone who is looking for your product or service, you need to persuade them to make a deal with *you*. The art of selling is about communicating with another human being. It's about you speaking directly to someone to whom you want to sell your ideas. In this case, you are explaining the reason why the seller should sell to you rather than market their property through an estate agent. You may, for instance, need to communicate to the seller that if they are behind with the mortgage, they need to act *now* before they get repossessed, and why going to an estate agent will not guarantee them a sale in time. It's your responsibility to ensure they understand that. There's always a chance they will sell their property in time by using an estate agent, but it's a *huge* risk and the downside of that risk is that their property could get repossessed. You have to show them that selling to *you*, a person offering them a guaranteed sale, is a much better idea.

There is a general negative perception about sales. People often say that they hate selling. Ask yourself "Do I like being sold to?" If the answer is no, then you are likely to not be a good salesperson.

However, my motto is: "In business, if you don't sell, you suck!" You have to make sales, or your business will not survive.

Selling doesn't have to be scary or unethical. If you knew that your children were mixing with the wrong people, would you not *sell* them the idea that they should stay away from those people? Or if you saw your friend in an abusive relationship, would you not *sell* the idea of getting out of it to them? Even if you are not aware of it, you do actually sell, all day and every day, without knowing it's selling.

I get people calling me and saying, "I lost my job, I'm behind on the mortgage, I've got some equity in the house, but I don't see a way out …". They are thinking about going to an estate agent. If I *know* that there is obviously no guarantee that the estate agent will sell the property in time, and if I *know* that I could guarantee this person a sale at a certain price, is it not ethical to "sell" that information to them?

For me, if you don't convince people, immediately, that their best option is certainly not an estate agent, then you are doing them a disservice. You have an obligation to explain to them that they should do a deal with you. If you don't explain this to them, and they go to the estate agent who tries and fails to sell their house (at any price) so they get repossessed, then, in my opinion, you have acted unethically.

What I have seen happen, again and again, is people burying their heads in the sand. They get into difficulties and they just assume everything will right itself someday. They do nothing; they freeze. Of course things don't get better, and they end up in a worse situation than ever. I don't want to think of that happening to anyone, which is why I will always try to help people.

Negotiation

As I've said before, negotiation skills are absolutely paramount to your success as a property entrepreneur. What I've noticed, in my years of teaching, is that people fall into two distinct groups:

1. People who think they are better negotiators than they really are (most people!).

2. People who think they can't negotiate at all.

I can teach both groups how to become better negotiators.

Negotiation is one of the earliest skills we learn as kids. Watch a seven-year-old boy negotiate with his mother about the time he's allowed to spend on the iPad, or a teenage girl negotiate with her father on what time she's allowed to come home from a party. Negotiation is basically the art of getting what you want, and it comes naturally to us at a very early age!

When it comes to negotiating property deals, however, there are some subtler notes to be aware of. The term "negotiation" has a harsh tone to it; I always say that it is more about **effective communication**. Most of it happens over the phone so you need to be comfortable speaking on the phone to people.

What you need to communicate to the seller is *why* he or she should listen to you in the first place. You need to build trust first, then you inform them and *then* you execute your offer. If they don't trust you, they won't listen to you. In fact, it goes even further back than that … they have to *like* you first. So, in order, you must ensure that:

1. You get them to like you.

2. You get them to trust you.

3. You inform them.

4. You then execute and close the deal.

This is not the same as closing a hard sale because you are getting to know the seller; you are building a relationship.

I once saw one of my most successful dealmakers talking on the phone. I didn't know who she was talking to, but from the way she was speaking it was obvious that it was one of her friends. She'd been sitting at her desk and she'd been chatting away for almost an hour. I got really annoyed that she was talking for so long to a friend during working hours. When she got off the phone I asked her: "Who was that you were talking to? You're meant to be working not gossiping with your friends." She told me it was a seller; she'd just closed a property deal. That's a great negotiator!

Since having that experience, I've always told people: "If you don't sound like you're talking to a friend, you're not doing it right."

Remember, it is not *what* you do but *how* you do it; it is not *what* you say but *how* you say it that matters most. You need to be aware of having the right tone, volume and energy in your voice. I teach negotiation skills at my property events and I always remember this one student who was a teacher. When she started negotiating she sounded like she was interrogating a misbehaving child! I had to teach her to be a little softer. It is important that you strike the right balance.

However, being too soft can also backfire. I have also seen people lose deals because they are very good at the relationship building part but then find that they can't close the deal; they haven't got the guts to cut to the chase and ask for it, even when things are going so well. Again it comes down to self-concept: you have to believe you deserve it. If you don't go in for the close, you give the seller too much time to think about it; the seller could easily talk himself out of it, or start listening to other people who try to talk him out of it. You can't wait too long before you go in to close the deal.

Again, don't be put off or become too deflated when the seller says "no". When you hear "no" you replace it with "Tell me more …".

The flip side of this is when everything feels too easy. This can just as easily make me nervous because I begin to worry about what the seller is not saying. I want all the objections to be out in the open. You even need to anticipate what the seller's objections might be before they say them.

The objections I most often hear are:

1. How do I know you are genuine/aren't trying to rip me off?

2. What are the hidden costs?

3. How do I know this is legal?

I immediately have answers to all these questions. I know my mental script. I even have a way to handle *any* objection that I teach to my students (this is the one part of my programme that everyone always loves!). We will be discussing how to handle objections in more detail in a forthcoming chapter.

At the end of the day, it is simply about understanding human nature and having empathy. These are the skills I perfected during my time as a pharmacist, through listening to the problems of people from every walk of life. I needed to develop a *huge* amount of empathy. I never imagined that my career as a pharmacist would give me some of the skills I needed to become a property investor.

If you're not a people person, you need to become one. That is, if you want to become a property entrepreneur!

The Systems Within The System

Your sales and marketing systems will produce leads. These are your potential deals. But of course the systemization doesn't stop there.

Now you have to analyse those potential deals, and finally apply dealmaking strategies to them. You can build a system to do that. So now you can see that there are smaller systems within the main system. It's like a computer; it's a network of related systems all working within one grand system.

Ultimately, property is a numbers game, so you need a system that churns out as many viable opportunities as possible.

The 100-10-5-3-1 Rule

For every deal you want to make, you need to start by analysing at least 100 potential deals. Chances are, you will find 10 that make your shortlist; that fit your criteria. You will probably make offers on five of those, three will accept and, of those, one will go through to completion. This is a development of the rule that property entrepreneur Dolf de Roos suggests.

So how do you find those 100 potential deals? Well, you don't go out looking for 100 *deals*; you go out looking for 100 *sellers*. You go out looking for people who want to sell their house, and out of those you will find your deals.

Many people who want to invest in property start out by knocking on estate agents' doors, going to auctions and searching websites. That's a very time-consuming and inefficient way of finding 100 sellers. It could then take you months to get to analyse them all. You may find some of your sellers this way, but we have to find a more efficient way of finding and assessing those 100 potential deals. When you truly get to grips with your system and know all the right questions to ask, you'll realize you don't even need to visit a property in order to assess it, you can do it all over the phone. (I now go one step further with my business and pay people to assess deals over the phone *for* me!) Remember, finding a BMV deal has very little to do with the property anyway, and everything to do with the seller's circumstances. You can get all that information by speaking with the seller over the phone.

Some people think that they have systemized their business because they analyse 100 properties online. Looking at information about properties online tells you nothing about the seller's circumstances, so you have no information upon which you can base your decision as to whether a property is a potential BMV deal. Remember, **one of the key determinants as to whether a property is a potential BMV deal is that there must be a** *motivated* **seller** and you can't tell if the seller is really motivated until you speak to them. You might be able to see the price of a property online, and maybe that price shows you that the property is technically under-valued, so if you have financing in place, great, you can go in and buy it. But most people don't have financing at their fingertips and the only way to buy (or rather control) property without financing is to negotiate the terms, and for that you need to be able to speak to the seller directly.

Your machine/system must give you all the relevant information you need; it must *qualify* potential deals it gives you to look at. The faster you can get and analyse those potential deals, the faster you can make your shortlist of 10 properties. The system must be designed to reduce the time it takes to find those potential deals to as short a time as possible.

Getting Qualified Leads Through Your System

So how do you design a system that *only* shows you properties from motivated sellers? The answer is simple. You create the marketing that attracts those sellers. That way you don't even need to go out and find the sellers, they come to you. So this is all about the **PULL** marketing that we discussed above. The start of your machine *is* your marketing system.

The next part of your system/machine is talking to the seller. The seller has come to you, through your pull marketing, saying that he is motivated to sell, but you need to speak to him directly and confirm this. Remember, a BMV deal is about the *terms* rather than a specific price. You will be offering a percentage below the valuation figure, and the terms under which you can make an offer. You can only negotiate these terms when you speak directly to the seller.

So what your system really needs to bring you is not 100 potential *properties*, it's 100 potential sellers, because **it is the seller's circumstances that qualify a property as a potential deal, not the property itself**.

Now you need to decide how many deals you'd like to get. Say in the coming year you'd like to do four property deals (that's one every three months), this means you need to be talking to 100 motivated sellers every three months, which is approximately 33 a month, or just over one seller a day. Let's call it seven sellers a week, as some days you might talk to two or three. In order to satisfy the 100-10-5-1 rule, you must be talking to seven sellers a week in order to get four deals per year. This is how a system works!

If those four deals a year are worth an average of £25,000 each (let's say you added two properties to your portfolio, adding a paper profit of £40,000 each, and flipped two properties to investors for fees of £10,000 each), then that would be an additional income of £100,000 per year. That's surely worth building a machine that keeps you talking to seven sellers a week!

My students often ask me, "How do you decide whether to keep a deal or flip it?" Well, when you build a property portfolio, you need to set criteria for the type of property you want to add to it. If a property doesn't meet your criteria, you should probably flip it rather than adding it to your portfolio. Your criteria can be anything, from price to location to all kinds of factors. For example, you might only want properties in your portfolio that are within a 10-mile radius of where you live, and that are also under £200,000 market value. You must still market to people whose properties fall outside those criteria because you can always flip a property deal to another investor. Say you live in Southampton and a seller contacts you who has a property in Glasgow that's worth £300,000; you can still do a deal (without even seeing the property) if the seller agrees to your price and terms. Then you flip it to another investor.

Setting Your Targets And Working Backwards

Some people have great aspirations but are not doing the necessary work to realize them. I always ask my students how many deals they want to do. I ask them what their *targets* are. If they say they want a portfolio of 20 properties within the next two years, I ask them how many sellers they have spoken to that week. If they say none, I explain that it is highly unlikely they are going to achieve their target of acquiring 20 properties in the next two years!

Work it backwards; if you want to acquire 20 properties in the next two years, that's 10 properties per year. Using the 100-10-5-1 rule, that means you need to analyse about 1,000 potential deals per year, which is just under 20 a week. You now know that you must build a machine that gives you 20 qualified motivated sellers to speak to each week.

But here's the good news.

You can *improve* those stats. Needing 100 qualified sellers to get one deal is just a rough guide. If you can improve your marketing so that it generates *better-qualified* leads, and if your negotiation skills are better than most people's, then you will improve those stats. Maybe you'll get two or three deals for every 100 qualified sellers you speak to rather than one. Maybe you'll even hit your target of acquiring 10 properties in the first six months of the year and go travelling for the second six months!

It's a simple formula:

QUALIFIED LEADS + GOOD NEGOTIATION SKILLS = PROPERTY DEALS

It then follows that:

BETTER-QUALIFIED LEADS + IMPROVED NEGOTIATION SKILLS = MORE PROPERTY DEALS

Let me show you how the machine works in practice. Even though I now hire people to do deals for me, when I was doing deals myself, this is what I would do.

I would wake up in the morning, do the school run, go to the gym and then go to a café with my laptop. I'd open my email and see messages from people who were keen to sell their properties quickly, who had seen my online advert promoting my services and had filled out the contact form. I would make an assessment of each person based on the answers to my carefully-worded qualifying questions (in the questionnaire they would have filled out when leaving their contact details). I would consider things like how quickly they needed to sell their property and what was their exact reason for needing a quick sale. I would rate these potential sellers and cherry-pick the ones I wanted to call. I'd sit in the café for about two hours and in that time I might talk to three or four sellers. I would do that five days a week. So I was talking to 15–20 sellers a week. That's a good quota. I would usually have a deal within about four to five weeks.

My system was well tuned to attract sellers, which meant I didn't have to go knocking on any doors or use middlemen. The system also filtered every applicant, by asking each one a series of questions. I kept honing those questions to ensure that I got better-qualified leads.

So the system starts with the online and offline marketing (Google ads, newspapers, leafleting, etc.) that drives traffic to your site. The marketing offers your services as an alternative and better option for selling houses quickly and assuredly than going through an estate agent. The next process in the system is a series of questions that a potential seller must answer when making their first enquiry, which qualifies them as a viable lead or not. If you are not getting the best leads, look at your questions – they may need adjusting. You could have the questions in an online questionnaire, or you could have a telephone number that people have to call and a call centre asking those same questions of potential leads.

When I call potential leads, I have another system that I adopt. This is my framework for the call; what I need to make sure I do during the call. This, again, is all systemized. I need to:

1. Gain their trust.

2. Get all the information I need from them.

3. Explain everything I could do to help them.

I need to make sure I cover these three things in the 30-minute call. Obviously some calls will be shorter because I might find that a seller is not as motivated as they made themselves out to be in the online questionnaire, or there is a problem with the property that I don't want to have to overcome, but generally, I take around 30 minutes to gain the seller's trust, get all the information I need and explain everything I could do for them.

Even if I do disqualify the seller after a few questions, I can still keep their details to follow up with them at a later date and find out if their situation has changed at all.

Say I get an enquiry from a Mrs Jones who says, in answer to one of my questions, that she urgently needs to sell her house as she has retired and is moving to Australia in two months time to live with her daughter; but when I call her and explain what I do and what my offer is, she says she's actually not in that much of a hurry and can actually wait up to a year. I politely explain that it doesn't sound like she needs my help right now, but I'll make a note to check back in with her in about nine months to see if she is still trying to sell her property and might need my help at that point. There's every chance that she may have had no luck with estate agents and is now desperate to move because her daughter is four months pregnant. At that point, if I help her get the house sold and everything done and dusted in six weeks, it will be a huge relief to her.

I have another system that automatically resends emails to people over the course of a year to ask them whether they are still trying to sell their house. If they get one of these each month while having no joy with the estate agents, chances are they will eventually contact me again.

So now you understand some of the core components of a successful value system. By now you should also fully appreciate that, if you want to be a successful property entrepreneur, you *have* to build a system. The problem for most people who try their hand at property investing is that they don't treat their endeavours as a *business.* So they don't consider building a system. But property is a business just like any other business, and the best way of maximizing your profits is to build a machine.

Servicing Your Systems

You must keep your overall system, and all the systems within it, well tuned. This will keep your costs down. Being able to qualify your leads over the phone, without even needing to see the property, means that you are not using up valuable money and time travelling around the country looking at properties. Also, with Skype and other Internet phone services, most phone calls these days are free, even international ones, as long as you have WiFi access.

You can confirm pretty much everything you need to know about a property and its seller over the phone. You want to collect as much information as you can before you go to visit the property – if you even go at all; I have bought and flipped plenty of properties that I have never seen. I have even systemized *this* step in the procedure by hiring someone else to view the property for me and produce a report for me. When you start out, obviously you need to view the properties yourself, but you can still get most of the information you need, such as the seller's specific motivation for selling, over the phone – you can even confirm the valuation over the phone and using the Internet by researching the market. Only when you have all the information you can possibly get, and you have agreed a price and terms, and – most importantly – have your lock-out agreement in place, are you ready to view the property. I see far too many investors driving around the country without lock-out agreements in place wasting their time because a) sellers too often change their minds and b) when you are doing BMV deals, it is too easy to get gazumped.

Gazumping basically means when the buyer and seller have agreed, verbally, on a price (after which time the buyer will proceed with the costly conveyancing process of commissioning a survey and instructing solicitors) and someone comes along and offers the seller a *higher* price, and the seller accepts that and pulls out of the original verbally agreed deal.

Of course, the best position of all to be in is to have a fully automated system.

Automating Your System

Before you can have a fully *automated* system, you need to know that your system actually works. Once your system is up and running, once it *is* actually working, you must start documenting every single thing you do. *Write everything down!* Literally, anything you do on a daily basis that leads you towards a property deal, write it down. This will eventually become your user manual for your future employees.

Be creative as you are working on building your system. Look at the best features of other people's systems and incorporate these features into your own system, or even improve on them. You have to consistently test and measure (put a method into action and look at your results, then change something in your method, put it into action again and see if you get better or worse results … keep doing this until you find the optimum method) to make sure your system is as effective as possible.

Once you have documented your system and have found the right components for it – which includes hiring the right people to run it – don't be afraid to start the machine up. I watch a lot of people spend too long on paper trying to build the perfect system without putting it into action. At some point you have to press play and see what happens. If your system doesn't work, fine; you'll figure out which bit doesn't work and you'll try again. But you'll never find out what doesn't work while it's all still on paper.

Your system is like a living, breathing organism that grows and changes. It adapts to new technology, it responds to changes in the market; it is always a work in progress. Life doesn't stand still and your system doesn't either. You can always tweak it … or pay someone to tweak it!

My Automated System

When I first set up my website, **NetworkPropertyBuyers**, I was still working as a pharmacist. I literally built my entire website on a little handheld PDA, tapping away, writing my copy, in between preparing prescriptions. Young people these days who are used to 3G and 4G speeds can't imagine what it was like with super slow GPRS connection … *all the time*! I love telling them my story. I always explain that it is a typical "no pain, no gain" story. When young people complain I tell them that there are no excuses. I was putting in 14-hour days as a pharmacist (including travel) and *then* working on building my business. I had no down time.

Now, I have worked my way into having a fully automated system. I don't think I've spoken to a seller in over five years (at time of writing). I have a team of expert negotiators who do that for me. It took me a long time to build my system and to fine tune every aspect of it, which included training people to work the way I work, but now I am just like the guy in the village who built the pipeline. I simply turn on the tap, sit back and enjoy the fresh water that flows into my reservoir!

I don't spend any time doing property deals anymore, but my property deals help fund my lifestyle and my other business endeavours. Now I get to do the things I am passionate about, like teaching, writing books, keeping fit, travelling the world and spending time with my wife and children.

I also spend time building new businesses because this is something I am passionate about. Once you've experienced the satisfaction of building one successful machine, you'll definitely want to do it again!

The difference between a person who says "I don't have time to build a business because of my job", and a person who is a multi-millionaire entrepreneur with multiple automated businesses, allowing him or her to do whatever they want with their time, is that the latter understands that, **to *make* more time in the long run, you have to *find* more time to invest in building your machine in the short term**. The guy who built the pipeline probably didn't sleep for three months while he built it (I know I missed out on many a night's sleep while building my business), but at the end of it all, he could sit back and enjoy his water with nothing more to do.

Laying that pipeline is HARD WORK! But the rewards will make it all worth it in the end. You might have to fix a few holes in your pipeline from time to time and upgrade some of your components, but this is all just maintenance; the machine will give you the results.

Always Adding Value

At the beginning of this section, I explained that when your **sales system**, **marketing system** and dealmaking **strategies** (which we will be learning all about in the next chapter) all work together efficiently as one system, we get **VALUE**. Yes, I *get* value but I also want to *add* value.

I know that what I am doing, ultimately, in my business, **is adding value to people's lives**. It's always got to be win-win for me. All my efforts, my whole machine – with its network of systems inside, my skill and knowledge – all come together to add value to my life and to other people's lives.

When someone desperately needs to sell their house, it is usually because their life has changed dramatically. Just imagine a man who loses his job when he has a wife and two young children to support. After a few months of using his savings and hunting for a new job to no avail, he has absolutely no way of keeping up with his mortgage payments. His parents have room to house the family for a year or so while the man gets back up on his feet, but what can he do about the house that he has a mortgage on? If he simply stops paying the mortgage, the bank will repossess the property. This will make it difficult for him to get another mortgage in the future, when things – hopefully – pick up for him again. Also, unlike in the United States where if a lender forecloses on a property they cannot pursue the previous owner for mortgage arrears (the reason why so many people walked away from properties posting the keys through the letter box in the financial crash), in the United Kingdom, lenders can go after the owner for arrears even after repossessing the property.

This man's situation has a negative impact on him and everyone around him. He suffers from stress thinking about his predicament, which negatively impacts his relationship with his wife and his children – who start to do badly at school. He isolates himself from his friends because he is too embarrassed to speak to them, and he stops taking care of himself, which has a negative impact on his health. He becomes obsessed with the fear of not knowing what will happen to him and can't sleep at night. The situation is terrible and only set to get worse.

I will do anything I can to help a person like that get rid of their property and get on with their lives. Obviously I am not a charity, I am a business so I need to make money, but in doing that I also help relieve this man of the burden that is causing him so much stress. I do so quickly and efficiently. I take my profit from the deal and he gets to move on with his life without the worry of what to do about the property that he cannot afford to pay for any more. People's lives are affected so dramatically when you help them like this. I have always found it incredibly rewarding.

When people like the man I have described above contact my company through my system, we start building a relationship with him and begin negotiations. We might even find a way of the seller getting something out of the deal that they weren't expecting; maybe a deferred payment that they will receive at some future date. That is because we treat them like a person and look at how we can add value to their lives while we also benefit. This wouldn't happen if the bank were to get there first and repossess the property. You can't imagine a bank saying: "Look, we're really sorry that we've got to repossess your house, but why don't we talk about it and see if we can do it while protecting you and getting something for you down the line." The bank is just going to take the house; they don't care. They don't treat the owner as a person, it is just a debt that has been defaulted on and they are calling in their insurance policy (taking the property). When I, or one of my negotiators, go in, we are looking at it from a different perspective: how can we both benefit from the deal? I'm always looking at where the seller might possibly be able to profit out of the deal as well as me, even if it's a long way down the line.

We will try to add value to people's lives no matter what the result of the negotiations. Even if we don't end up doing a deal with people, we will give them the best advice we can offer them. When I was a pharmacist, if I felt someone was going to buy some expensive medicine that they didn't need, I would tell them. I couldn't see someone spending unnecessary money.

So even if we lose a sale, we still create *good will*. **This comes from a genuine desire to add value to people's lives**. This is what motivates me!

But it's not just motivated sellers and my business that I am adding value to, I also add value to other property investors who want to do deals but don't have the time or the know-how to source deals. I add value to someone's business when I flip them a deal. Yes, I get paid too, but the bottom line is they benefit from my expertise. If I flip a deal to an investor worth £40,000 in equity and they pay me £10,000, I get my money but I have added great value to the investor's portfolio by helping them gain £40,000 in equity (for the price of £10,000). The investor didn't physically do anything at all, except take my phone call and read and agree to the terms of the deal.

Add into the mix the seller who has been able to get rid of their property and get on with their life and you have a win-win-*win* situation!

Win-Win-Win

Let's look at a great example of a win-win-win situation.

Say that a seller's property is worth £200,000. He has a mortgage of £100,000 on it (having originally bought it for £120,000 six years ago, putting down a deposit of £15,000 and having paid off £5,000). The owner is desperate to release the equity to invest it in a business. He needs that money within two months or the business opportunity will disappear. I offer him £160,000. This will give him £60,000 cash in a guaranteed space of time – say six weeks – allowing him to invest in the business opportunity he's passionate about. Sure, he could put the property on the market with an estate agent and maybe, if he's lucky, he'd get an offer of £190,000. If he's even luckier, the sale will go through a day or so before he needs to invest in the business deal. But figuring that "a bird in the hand is worth two in the bush" he takes my offer and sleeps easy at night! In this scenario, I don't want to add the property to my portfolio, so I go to an investor who has cash to invest. The investor pays me £10,000 and buys the property for a further £160,000, giving him an instant on-paper profit of £30,000 (because he's got a place worth £200,000 for £170,000), which is a 300% ROI. The seller gets his £60,000 in time to make his investment, and it's win-win-win. A great day for all!

In fact, it can go even further than that.

Let's say the investor is a student of mine who wants to add value to a tenant. He wants to help the tenant get on the property ladder. He could rent the property to the tenant over a seven-year period on the basis that the tenant has the right to buy at a price you fix today, say £230,000 (remember, the likelihood is that the property will be worth considerably more than £230,000 in seven years). In exchange for the right to buy the property at this price in seven years and the peace of mind that he can treat the property as his own and renovate it – i.e. treat it as a home and not a rental, the tenant is willing to pay a premium rent (say £800 per month instead of £600 per month). The investor benefits from the extra rental and a guaranteed tenant for seven years. The tenant benefits from the guarantee that he will be on the property ladder in seven years' time for a fixed price; yes he's paid extra rental and a fee to the investor for the deal, but this will be a fraction of what he would need to put down as a deposit.

This looks like a win-win-win-*win* to me!

8

Seven Dealmaking Strategies

Now comes the part of the book you've all been waiting for ... when I give away all my best-kept secrets! Why do I want to do this? Because I can't possibly service all the potential property deals out there myself, and the more people who learn to do deals this way, ethically and successfully, the better the property business will become for everyone!

A key point that I want you to keep in mind throughout as you learn about these strategies is that it is *not* a "one-size-fits-all" situation. When you are dealing with motivated sellers (the only type of seller we deal with as property entrepreneurs), you are dealing with idiosyncratic situations. Each motivated seller will have particular needs. The great advantage of knowing and understanding several different strategies is that you have choices. You may need to combine a couple of these strategies (say use a mortgage host when you are also doing a lease-option deal) but you will always have choice. Who knows, you may even come up with a new strategy yourself. I hope, if you do, you'll come and share it with me!

I have **SEVEN STRATEGIES** that I have used myself, which are all based on the **negotiation of terms** and are suitable for ordinary non-cash-rich people who want to be on the property ladder. These are the seven strategies every property entrepreneur should know, inside out and back to front:

1. Tenancy In Common.

2. Mortgage Hosting.

3. Options.

4. Lease-Option Deals.

5. Rent-To-Buy.

6. "Bob The Builder."

7. Part Now, Part Later.

Tenancy In Common

If you cannot qualify for a traditional mortgage – usually because you don't have the salary or credit history to support it – you can use the **Tenancy in Common** strategy. To do this, you need to find another person (most likely a friend or relative, but it could be another investor) who *can* qualify for a mortgage (or with whom you can jointly qualify for a mortgage) and apply for a mortgage together. In this scenario, both your names will be on the title deeds to the property. You can use this strategy either to buy an investment property as a buy-to-let, or to buy your first residence. The advantage being that it helps you get onto the property ladder with a first mortgage in your name (albeit jointly with another person). Your share of the property doesn't have to be a straight 50:50 split; it can be anything from 1–99%. The idea is just to get your foot through the mortgage door.

Buy-To-Let Mortgages

This is a good time to talk about buy-to-let mortgages.

You may be surprised to hear that specific "buy-to-let" mortgages only really exist in the UK. In most countries, lenders will not give you a mortgage if you want to use it to acquire a property that you intend to rent out. This is what makes the UK such a haven for property investors. Once you have one mortgage, you can actually have several buy-to-let mortgages in your name, as long as you have the salary to qualify for the initial mortgage, i.e. you would need a salary of say £30,000+ to qualify for a mortgage of around £90,000–120,000 in the first place – you can usually borrow three to four times your salary – but after that, you can get mortgages for several properties – usually up to seven or eight as long as you have the required deposit. It is not that you can borrow up to a total multiple of your salary, rather that your salary can alone underwrite multiple buy-to-let mortgages as long as you have a deposit for each one. In fact, at one time, before the global financial crisis shone the spotlight on the subprime mortgage market, there was no limit on the number of buy-to-let mortgages you could have under these criteria. These days most lenders in the UK restrict you to seven or eight, as I mentioned, but the number does tend to fluctuate year to year depending on the state of the economy. In most other countries of the world, they will lend you up to a certain multiple of your income and that is it. So, say you earn £50,000, you can usually borrow around £200,000, but that's all. You can usually only borrow (in total) a small multiple of your income. The exact level of your borrowing is tied to your income level.

In the UK, at the time of writing, you can even get buy-to-let mortgages that are interest only. These are mortgages where you only pay the annual interest (on a monthly basis).

To the best of my knowledge, buy-to-let mortgages are only available in the UK; in the rest of the world, you have to buy investment properties for cash. If you have a mortgage it is normally illegal to rent out your property without permission from the mortgage lender. People will often sublet illegally instead of going through the hassle of applying for permission. In the Netherlands, as you will see demonstrated in the case studies towards the end of this book, it is particularly difficult to get permission from mortgage lenders to rent out your property. Most people in Holland try to get into the position where they own their properties outright specifically so that they can do what they want with it.

And as I've said before, UK landlords are further incentivized by having the law very much on their side, thanks to the Assured Short-hold Tenancy agreement (this is the case in England and Wales by the way, the Scottish version is similar but is called the Short Assured Tenancy.) This basically gives landlords the right to give tenants a two-month notice period after the first six months of any tenancy agreement. In the rest of the world, tenants have many more rights and can effectively become "sitting tenants" where, as long as they continue to pay their rent, it is very difficult to evict them. Lenders obviously do not like this situation, because if the mortgage holder stopped paying the mortgage for any reason, it makes it extremely difficult to evict the tenants and foreclose on the property to recoup the loan. This is why the rest of the world is not so lenient when it comes to buy-to-let loans.

All these factors point to why the UK hugely favours investors, while many other countries don't.

However, if you want to get a buy-to-let mortgage, you should first focus on getting a residential mortgage. Most lenders in the UK won't consider you for a buy-to-let mortgage if you don't have a residential mortgage. We have previously looked at how the figures don't add up to allow regular people on a regular salary to save enough in any reasonable length of time to get a deposit together, which is why the "Tenancy in Common" strategy is such a good one for getting people their first residential mortgage with a view to progressing to a buy-to-let mortgage.

Mortgage Hosting

As with the "Tenancy In Common" strategy, here you will need to find someone – ideally a close friend or relative – who will take out a mortgage in their name (and potentially even supply the deposit), and will make a separate contract with you to deed a certain percentage of the proceeds of the property (either the capital gains or the cash flow, or a mix of both) so that you are a beneficiary of the property without your name being on the title or the mortgage. Why would they do this for you? Because you brought them the deal in the first place, and maybe you've offered to manage the property.

Of course this strategy doesn't help you get onto the property ladder *per se*, but it *is* a way of making money from property and that, as property entrepreneurs, is the name of the game!

Most people, when I first suggest "Tenancy In Common" or "Mortgage Hosting" to them, are convinced that they do not have anyone in their lives who would be in a position to help them. However, once we talk further it turns out that they *do* know someone in this position; they just don't want to ask. Don't rule anything out. You have to be able to ask; you never know when you might hear a "yes". Make a list of everyone you know well who has property, who has some asset-based wealth, and ask each of them whether they would be prepared to host a mortgage for you and help you put a deposit together (that they are able to lend you in the long term and that you hope you will be able to repay with interest eventually). If you are afraid of them judging you or thinking badly of you for asking, you obviously don't trust their friendship or affection for you. If they are genuine friends and care about you, they will respect you for asking, even if they have to say "no".

You might find someone who is able to guarantee your mortgage but can't give you a deposit. Then you can go back to the idea of finding a deal, i.e. find a below market value property that you can buy so that there is instant paper profit. You can then go and enter into a "deed of trust" agreement with your friend. You will share the profit 50:50 or whatever percentage you want to offer.

The Bank Of Mum And Dad (Or Your Equivalent Fan Club!)

If you want to start investing in property but you don't have a deposit or eligibility for a mortgage, your first and best option is to ask a family member or close friend to gift you a deposit and get a joint mortgage in both your names. This is particularly common practice these days for young people. The banks really don't like lending to young people. This way, you will get a credit history. And if you play your cards right, you will probably be able to pay your family member back, with interest, in around five years or so.

This is also a great way in which parents can reduce their inheritance tax. UK tax law allows you to give away a certain amount to your children NOW so that there is less for them to inherit (and pay tax on) down the line. Obviously there is not a lot for them to gain from this, but they are doing it to help you, not to make money. However, it is *still* an investment so it's not like there is no potential profit to be made. You still need to sell the benefits to your benefactors! There could be some profit in it, just not a quick gain.

This strategy is very much about *you* and what is best for you. They have the security of the actual property. Remember one of the golden rules in sales is ABC (Always Be Closing). Even if you're selling to your parents, you still need to sell the idea to them and explain why it's such a good idea. This shouldn't be too hard; most of us have been selling ideas to our parents since we were kids – selling to them why you *must* have that new bike or phone, etc. Why stop now?

Options

I'm now going to give you an overview of what option agreements are all about and how they can be put into effect to facilitate property deals. This will also enable you to understand the further four strategies in this chapter, which are all versions of option agreements.

The concept of **option agreements** is not a new one; it has been an instrument in the financial markets for years. Investors buy and sell stock options all the time.

Option agreements are also commonly used in the entertainment industry. If a film or television production company wants to purchase the right to adapt a book or article (which is the intellectual property of the author), they usually put into place an option agreement, which gives them the *exclusive right* (but not obligation) to purchase that intellectual property within a certain time frame. They will normally pay a fee, which is a percentage (and portion) of the agreed purchase fee. You may hear, for example, of a major film studio paying $50,000 against $500,000 for the option to turn a very popular novel into a film. That means they pay the author $50,000 up front and the remaining $450,000 when the film is given the "green light" (i.e. all the funding is in place and pre-production is about to start). If, within the option period (say it is five years), the studio does not exercise its option to make the film, the author is free to sell the intellectual property rights to someone else.

Option agreements have also been used as an instrument in commercial real estate for years, to purchase land and property for development. However, until I started doing it, no one in the UK had tried to use option agreements as an instrument for buying property in the residential market. Why? I can only assume that it was believed that your average person wasn't savvy enough to understand the complexity of an option agreement. It's my personal opinion that the general public are kept in the dark by governments and financial institutions. Everything is dumbed down and served up like baby food – easily digestible for everyone. But you're not a baby! You deserve to know all the *options* available to you.

Remember, it is in your estate agent's interest that you do not know how to negotiate your own deals. The estate agent makes money out of you *not* knowing how to negotiate. That is money *you* could use!

Put simply, if you learn to negotiate in place of an estate agent, you will benefit.

Similarly, mortgage lenders do not want you to know how to negotiate a deal that will allow you to control a property without a mortgage for several years because that's several years' worth of interest they won't be getting!

When I realized how badly people were being kept in the dark, after I successfully negotiated my first option-based deal for a residential property, I became determined to educate people, to tell them about all the unconventional ways in which they could become property investors. I was frustrated by seeing people struggle to save enough for a deposit, or get rejected for a mortgage on the grounds that they were too young. I wanted people to know all the opportunities that were available to them. Nothing angers me more than an elitist system that shuts out the newcomer.

Put simply, an option is a **period of time** – a "window" so to speak – during which **the price of something is fixed and you have the right *but not the obligation* to buy it at that fixed price**. The terms of that option agreement can be whatever the two parties making the deal want them to be.

In every option deal, there is a **GRANTOR** or "**optioner**" (the giver of the option, the seller) and a **GRANTEE** or "**optionee**" (the buyer, the recipient of the option). There is also a specified **OPTION PERIOD** during which the grantee, the holder of the option, can exercise his or her right to buy the property *at any time*. The option period with property options can be anything from three months to many years (often being specifically the length of time left on a mortgage). This is slightly different from the way options work in the financial markets. With stock options, the option period is typically quite short – usually three, six or nine months – and the grantee cannot exercise their right to buy the commodity until the *end* of that period. In property, the grantee can exercise their option at any time. It usually behooves them to wait until the end of the option period in order to maximize their profit (assuming property prices are rising steadily), but there may be a time when prices have taken a sharp rise and they decide to exercise their option. For example, if you have a seven-year option to buy a property for £200,000, and after only three years the value of the property has gone up to £240,000, that's a good profit and it might be that you decide to "cash in" and exercise your option in case prices slip again. Compare this flexibility to the rigidity of stock options. If you have a three-month option to buy coffee at a fixed price, and after two months the price suddenly shoots up, you can't take advantage of that. You have to wait until the end of the three months, at which point the price may have come down. It may even have crashed! (There are some variables to fixed option periods on stock options where you *can* structure it so that you have more flexibility, particularly in the US, but generally this is how they operate, and I'm just using the regular model to highlight the flexibility of property options.)

Remember, of course, that the property market moves much slower than the stock market, which is why you will benefit from a *longer* option period as well as the *flexibility* to get out whenever you want.

The bottom line is, with any option agreement in property, you are free to negotiate whatever you want. There is no "standard" option contract for buying property. This is a **new type of property deal** and, as long as you educate yourself and ensure you understand every aspect of the deal, you can negotiate whatever you can.

Incidentally, I really want to stress this point about education. I would not be where I am today had I not attended countless courses and invested in training. Find out what your weak areas are and brush up on your skills. For instance, if you're not great at negotiating, go and take a negotiation course. If you don't understand how to value property, attend a course. How will you ever know if you have a true BMV deal unless you can assess the true value of a property? Go to real, live events and courses. You'll never gain enough knowledge and experience from reading a book or watching online content.

At this point you may ask (as I am constantly asked): *why would the seller give me an option in the first place?* This is a very good question. On the face of it, an option agreement does seem to massively favour the grantee (buyer) because his or her potential benefit is unlimited, whereas the grantor (seller) technically has potential unlimited loss (if you consider anything that the grantee makes *could* have belonged to the grantor). Furthermore, the grantee/buyer could walk away and not buy it at the end of the option period. So ... what's in it for the grantor? Well, usually it's the relief of relinquishing the responsibility for a property and any mortgage payments on it, plus the guarantee of the final sale down the line.

Most people assume that when someone wants to sell a property, it is all about making a profit. But this is not the case for every seller. Sometimes the seller has more pressing needs than making a profit. Always remember ... **it is the discovery and understanding of those needs that puts the grantee (buyer) in the best position to negotiate**. If a person urgently needs to be free of the obligations of their property, work with them to figure out how you can help them, in a way that helps you too!

Now let's look at some of the applications of options – under which circumstances an option agreement can be useful. We will also go through some of the different elements of an option agreement.

Short-Term Option Contracts

One of the most fundamental uses of an option deal is to prevent gazumping (where another buyer comes in after you'd agreed a price with the seller and undercuts your price, thereby "stealing" the deal from you).

In the UK, this is most relevant in England, Wales and Northern Ireland. In Scotland, because of the difference in the way offers are made and conveyancing takes place, gazumping is rare.

In property, an option agreement can also be referred to as a **lock-out agreement** since it effectively locks anyone else out from doing a deal on the property. One of the most straightforward applications of option agreements in property, therefore, is to stop anyone from gazumping you. Using an option agreement (lock-out agreement), you can ensure that you **never get gazumped again**!

Technically, gazumping is not illegal because when you make an offer on a property it is always "subject to contract" – i.e. until you have something in writing, either party can pull out, and in most cases you would not exchange contracts until a full structural survey and land searches, etc. have been carried out. This incurs costs for the buyer. There are also costs involved in processing the mortgage paperwork and getting the money in place. In general, there is a lot of risk involved for a buyer before contracts are exchanged. During this time there is nothing to stop the seller from continuing to market the property and look for a higher price for it, especially if house prices are on the up!

Why isn't it common practice for the buyer to obtain a binding contract before spending any money? Perhaps because it's in no one else's best interests. Think about it … if the estate agent can get a better price in the interim, he or she gets more money, as does the buyer. The surveyors and solicitors are not exactly going to turn down work. It is in no one but the *buyer's* interest to get a binding contract to protect against gazumping … and that's where understanding how to use an option agreement could save you money!

And let's face it … why *shouldn't* you be protected? If you are beginning to invest in the purchasing process, it makes absolute sense and seems completely fair to be protected. When you think about it, it seems ludicrous that it is standard practice in the UK *not* to have a lock-out agreement in place! I believe the only reason people don't get one is because they literally don't know they have the right to ask for it. Hopefully the information I'm offering in this book will change all that.

Obviously, the most important situation in which you need a lock-out agreement is when you have a BMV deal. If you've negotiated a particularly large discount on a property, you are more vulnerable to gazumpers.

So how long should a standard lock-out agreement be for? Typically it takes three months to complete a property purchase. If you agree a price with a seller and you want to protect yourself from being gazumped, a three-month option contract is the perfect way to do that. A **short-term option contract** gives you the exclusive right (but no obligation) to buy the property at an agreed price.

Why would a seller give you a lock-out agreement? Well, most importantly, they would only give you a lock-out agreement if speed and a guaranteed sale are more important than profit to them – i.e. they *must* be a **motivated** seller (as per our first golden rule). Again, my blanket advice to all property entrepreneurs is **never deal with sellers who are not motivated**. If a seller is not motivated, why would they give you a below market value price or protection while you go through the conveyancing process? Only a serious seller, who is fairly desperate to be free of his or her obligations and responsibilities on a property, will give you a price that offers you a decent paper profit *as well as* the protection you need while you complete the purchase.

Option Fees

You typically pay a fee for an option agreement. When this is a short-term agreement, the fee will be nominal, usually around £1, although you could increase it if you needed to add some incentive to the seller. When you negotiate an option agreement for a longer time period, the fee will usually be more significant. Indeed, if there is potential for a particularly large profit, the fee could seem quite high, but then it's proportional to the potential reward, for example property development.

Let's imagine there's a property entrepreneur called Chris who finds a piece of land and approaches the owner about buying it. At the time, the land has no planning permission, but Chris is an expert at planning applications. He offers the owner a £10,000 option fee for a two-year option to buy the land for £100,000. Chris has calculated that the GDV (Gross Development Value) of the land is around £2 million, which means he should be able to sell the land *with* the permission (note the permission stays with the land, not the applicant) to a developer for around £500,000. Thus, even after paying for the whole application process – which may cost him in the region of £40,000–50,000 for the all the services of the architects, consultants and engineers he needs to engage, and the reports that have to be commissioned – he stands to make a nice profit of around £350,000.

Of course there is a high risk here because, if Chris had not obtained his planning permission in the two-year period, he would have lost his £10,000 fee plus whatever fees he has paid out during the planning application process. He might lose as much as £60,000. You want a big reward? You have to take a big risk!

Option fees vary. You legally have to pay a consideration fee, but it can be anything from £1 to £20,000 or more.

If you want to pay a very low option fee up front, you can offer the owner a percentage of the profit instead. Chris could say to this developer: "Give me a two-year option agreement for £1 to buy this land and I will apply for planning permission. If I get it and am able to get an offer for the land plus planning permission from a developer, I'll give you 20% of the profit." Now, if Chris makes his £350,000, the seller of the land will make £70,000. That will eat into his profit but it reduces his up-front risk.

The key thing to remember is that when you are negotiating an option agreement, you have a huge amount of flexibility. Everything is negotiable.

Option-driven Leverage

An option agreement gives you enormous control. When you pay a relatively small fee (compared to the potential profit you could make) for an option agreement, you have a huge amount of leverage. Remember: the goal is all about control. When you have an option agreement, you have complete control over a potentially hugely valuable piece of real estate.

Leverage is what you get when laying out a relatively small amount of money or effort allows you to control a much larger asset.

Remember: leverage is minimum effort giving you maximum result.

The option agreement is actually a derivative instrument that gives you leverage. If you hold the exclusive right (but not obligation) to purchase a property at 30% BMV (say a paper profit of around £60,000), and you've only paid a £1 option fee and a few hundred pounds in conveyancing fees ... that's a highly-leveraged asset!

Lease-Option Deals

The Lease-Option strategy for acquiring property is, as I've explained before, my baby. I was the pioneer of applying this strategy to residential property deals. Thanks to my tireless efforts, this strategy for acquiring property is now legal in the UK, Scotland, the Netherlands, Malaysia and more countries soon to be accounted.

If you've understood how the basic option deal works, as applied to property, you're half way to understanding how lease-option deals work.

What Does The Lease-Option Agreement Consist Of?

There are basically two distinct parts to a lease-option agreement.

Firstly there is the **option agreement** that is just like any other option agreement, except it will be for a considerable length of time, usually between five and twenty years (typically covering the remaining mortgage term). As with any option agreement, you have to pay a fee but only a nominal one, normally £1. Under the option agreement you will have the right to buy that property at an agreed price at any time during the option period. You may or may not agree to split the profit you make with the seller (this might depend on the size of the fee you are offering up front).

The second part of the lease-option agreement is the **lease agreement**. Until such time as you exercise your option to *buy* the property, you will effectively be *leasing* the property by covering the seller's monthly mortgage payments, as well as taking responsibility for all associated expenses on the property, such as utility bills and maintenance/repair costs. Under this agreement you are entitled to rent the property out to a tenant and keep any profit you make on your rental income.

At this point you might ask if the seller needs the lender's permission to lease the property to you (the seller is then at liberty to allow you to sublet the property out again). The answer is, yes, most mortgage terms do state that the owner must get the lender's permission to rent the property out, but in my experience very few lenders will ever refuse permission. They have to give a very good reason why they won't grant their permission. On the few occasions I've had a lender not grant permission, I've contested this and managed to get the decision reversed. Most residential lenders in the UK are regulated by the FCA (Financial Conduct Authority) and are therefore bound to treat their customers fairly, so if they refuse permission to rent the property out without giving a good reason, you can challenge them. In the end, all the lender wants is to receive the mortgage repayments made. If the owner has demonstrated that he or she is unable to meet these payments without renting the property out, then the lender does not have a fair reason to refuse permission.

A lease-option deal basically allows the seller to negotiate terms with the buyer where they end up in a situation where it is *as if* the seller has sold the property (because they are no longer responsible for paying the mortgage or any other liability associated with the property). Looking at it another way, it's also like having a long-term tenant who is going to do all the maintenance on the property and guarantees paying their rent on time until the end of the mortgage term!

Seller Circumstance Driven

The relevance of this strategy, i.e. whether it is the appropriate strategy for you to use, will depend largely on the seller's circumstances.

Say you met a seller and they were desperate to sell their property because they had been made redundant, or had inherited a mortgaged property in poor condition and didn't have the available funds to make it habitable to rent out *or* cover the mortgage on it. If there is not much equity in the property (or worse, negative equity), then they are in a really tough situation. Maybe people in this situation end up letting the lender repossess the property because they think they have no other choice. Things may even turn from bad to worse because, if there are any mortgage arrears, the lender can then come after the seller to recover that money.

However, if you (the buyer) could offer the seller a win-win solution, there could be a positive outcome for everyone.

A lease-option deal can be a true gift for a motivated seller in this type of situation. If the buyer/investor can take over the mortgage and all the financial responsibilities associated with the property from day one, a seller can move on with his or her life without the burden of a mortgage and bills to pay.

Always remember:

> **One person's liability is another person's asset!**

You may ask, "Why doesn't the seller just move out and rent the property out to a tenant themselves?" That's a valid question, but not all sellers are able or want to take on that kind of responsibility. People who are in a really difficult situation usually just want to have everything handled for them. They simply want to move on with their lives, and they are willing to trade potential profit in return for having everything dealt with smoothly and efficiently for them. Renting out a property takes time and money. Sellers in circumstances such as those we are talking about here have neither. Becoming a landlord is stressful at the best of times; someone in a desperate situation probably couldn't deal with that stress (otherwise they would have done it already and wouldn't *be* in the desperate situation they are in).

While most lease-option deals are driven by the seller's circumstances, there will be occasions when this strategy is driven by the buyer's circumstances. For instance, if the buyer does not qualify for a mortgage or doesn't have a deposit, but understands how to structure a lease-option deal and can also manage a property (while perhaps the owner is not an experienced or willing landlord), then a lease-option deal would be a good choice for both parties.

The Negative Equity Trap

Negative equity (when the outstanding amount of your mortgage loan is more than the current value of the property) is not a problem, *per se*, if the seller is able to keep up the mortgage payments. But if they can't, they are not in a position to sell, either, because they would then owe the bank the balance of their mortgage. If you borrowed £180,000 to buy a house that was once worth £200,000, and the value of that house drops to £170,000 and that's all you could get for it, if you sold it, you'd owe the bank a lump sum of £10,000. If you need to sell because you can't keep up the mortgage repayments, you obviously don't have £10,000 sitting around to give to the bank!

I have always felt bad for people who get into a negative equity situation. Property goes in cycles, in waves, with boom and bust periods. During the boom years people often get overexcited and borrow too much money against the inflated value of a property. When prices drop they can find themselves in negative equity. If their circumstances render them unable to keep up their mortgage repayments during this period of being in negative equity, they are in a really desperate situation ... stuck between the proverbial rock and hard place. We saw countless people get into difficulties after the global economic crash of 2007–08 because they had borrowed too much in the boom years.

For people in negative equity, the lease-option deal can feel like an absolute lifesaver. This deal gives them an immediate way out. They can stop paying the mortgage and all their bills immediately (the same result as instantly selling the property). Even though they still technically own it on paper, they will have no more responsibility for it. In some circumstances they even stand to gain instant cash (from the fee that the buyer will give them for the option) and a little long-term profit (because most buyers in this situation will offer the seller a percentage of whatever profit the buyer makes when he or she exercises the option to buy at what will be, at the time, well below the market value and then sells the property on for a profit).

Exercising The Option

When the time comes for the buyer to exercise his or her option (either during or at the end of the option period), it is always possible for the buyer to "flip" or "assign" that option to another investor, especially if the buyer does not qualify for a mortgage for any reason. The buyer will not exercise the option until there is a substantial profit to be made (i.e. a good gap between the price the buyer has the option to buy at and the market value). There will never be a problem selling such a deal on to another investor because the on-paper profit will be substantial.

In this scenario, you would have three individual parties:

1. The **original owner** who granted the lease option to the initial investor; the **grantor**. The owner will still hold the deeds to the property and, although they have had no financial obligations on the property, they may be due a small share of the profit if the buyer has granted that in the terms of the deal.

2. The **original buyer** who negotiated the deal and has been paying the mortgage (out of the rental income he or she is receiving on the property) for a considerable period of time. This person holds the right to buy the property at a price that should be significantly below the market value of the property by the end of the option period.

3. A **third-party investor** who is going to buy this deal from the original buyer. This could be, as I said, because the original buyer is unable to get a mortgage when they decide to exercise their option. (Note: there could be many reasons why a person ends up unable to get a mortgage. Some property investors end up with too many mortgages and the bank won't give them anymore. Part of being a **property entrepreneur** is getting around this by flipping the deal to another investor who is cash-rich or able to get a mortgage.)

Ultimately, remember that if you have *control* of a property that you have the *right but no obligation* to buy at a *considerably discounted price*, then **you are in a very strong position**.

The Lease-Option Contract

To be able to negotiate lease-option agreements securely and successfully, you must have what I call the "5 Cs". These are:

The Concept You need to be absolutely watertight on the concept. You will be explaining a new concept to people, you must understand it inside out and back to front before you start suggesting it to others. Read and re-read the information in this book and make sure you are well educated on the concept. Ideally, shadow someone else making a lease-option agreement before you try it on your own.

The Contract You must understand the whole legal framework in order to negotiate a lease-option deal. You need to find an open-minded lawyer who will work with you to produce the right contract. Look for a lawyer with commercial real estate experience; they will be a safer bet than those who have dealt exclusively with residential real estate because they will at least understand the concept of lease-options. Don't be put off (or surprised!) if you hear some negative responses from the first few lawyers you speak to. Don't argue with them, just politely thank them for their time and move on. It's not worth the hassle of trying to convince negative, closed-minded lawyers that this is a great strategy. Just keep going until you find the right lawyer, someone who is going to work with you positively, who either has experience dealing with commercial real estate or who says, "I've not heard of using lease-option deals to buy residential property before, but it sounds interesting so let me take a look and then let's talk further". Again, *you* must understand the concept before you go looking for a lawyer. Remember, lawyers are expensive and charge by the hour.

The Circumstances As I mentioned at the beginning of the chapter, this strategy (as with every strategy) is not one-size-fits-all. You must understand the different situations in which using a lease-option deal would be applicable. A lease-option deal is not right for every scenario. For example, if a seller has a large chunk of equity in a property and simply wants to release it fast, a lease-option deal would not normally be appropriate. Here, you simply need to use a straight BMV offer in exchange for a four-week completion. And don't imagine that you can just "go out looking for a lease-option deal". It doesn't work like that. You go out looking for deals, armed with a selection of "tools", a lease-option agreement being one of those tools. You must know exactly the right scenario under which to suggest your lease-option tool. Your journey as a property investor has a particular path. First you create leads; from your many leads you find some potential deals; when you've identified your potential deals, you pick out the strategy you think will fit best to acquire (control) it; and then you negotiate with the seller. (We will come back to this journey and expand on it in a later section.) Never put the cart before the horse. You don't fit the circumstances to the tool; you fit the tool to the circumstances. Look at your circumstances before you choose your tool.

Every seller is different. Every situation is different. You must always make informed decisions.

Customization   Every lease-option contract will be bespoke, even if there are many similarities between them, because every seller's circumstances are unique. You can negotiate whatever terms you want, but these will be unique to each situation. The contract has to be customized to every individual situation. Just as is the case with the strategies themselves, when it comes to the contract, it's not a case of one size fits all. Each deal is dependent on the individual circumstances of the seller. You can't use a pro forma contract. You can draw from previous lease-option contracts, but each contract will be unique and specific to you, your seller and the property.

Communication   It is *vital* that you communicate well with your seller. You will most likely be introducing them to a concept they have never heard of before. You must know how to handle all their objections (a list of which is coming soon). Remember another golden rule: **if you confuse them, you will lose them**. You must understand every part of the concept and know exactly what you are offering before you start speaking about a lease-option agreement. If you walked up to a seller (particularly a highly-stressed seller who is about to be evicted) and you say, "Here's what we can do … you grant me the no-obligation right to purchase your property at a pre-agreed price date for the next ten years. I'll pay you a nominal fee of £1 for this and take over all your mortgage payments and liabilities so that you are free to move on", the seller is likely to call you crazy and slam the door in your face! (I can assure you of this from direct experience, as I will share anon …)

Dealing With The Seller's Questions

Obviously, for most people, a lease-option deal is something completely new, so they will have many concerns and questions. Here are some examples of questions I've been asked, and how to answer them:

1. How do I know this is legal?

Answer: Because everything will be in a contract that is drawn up by established lawyers. Lawyers cannot sign off on anything that is illegal.

2. What if you stop paying my mortgage?

Answer: When we agree on the option period, unless I exercise my option to buy (in which case, you get the money for the property and the mortgage is paid off), I am legally bound to pay your mortgage for the entire option period. If I stop paying then I would be in breach of contract; you would gain immediate control of the property as security and could take me to court for any losses. But this is also a reason why you should only do a deal like this with a reputable company. (Of course, you might now argue that, as a fledgling property entrepreneur, you are not a "reputable company" yet. But it's like with any business, when you are starting out, if you want to use this strategy, you must partner up with an investor who has experience of doing a lease-option deal in order to give yourself real weight and credibility until you have built your own reputation.)

3. What if you decide *not* to buy my house at the end of the option period?

Answer: First of all this is *highly* unlikely. Because even if I decide I don't want to buy it myself, there will be enough equity in it that it would make no financial sense to walk away from it. At the very least I would flip it to another investor. I would have to be very foolish, after paying the mortgage for all that time, not to exercise my option. However, if for some reason I did walk away and the house went back to you, you'd be getting a huge bonus because you'd get to keep all that equity yourself. Plus, the chances are your situation will have changed considerably and you will be able to manage the property in a way that you were unable to before.

4. Do you only buy my house at the end of the option period?

Answer: No, I can buy any time *during* the option period, but it will make no difference to you. I'm "babysitting" your mortgage and taking over all your maintenance so it's like you don't own the house anyway. The only possible *benefit* to you if I buy earlier than the end of the option period is if we have an equity-share deal (where I have agreed to give you a portion of the profit I make when I buy the house); you would simply get this early … so it's a *bonus* to you! One situation where this might happen is if, for example, I only have one year left of my option period and there is a sudden boom in the property market. I might decide to buy at what I anticipate is the top of the market rather than a year later when prices might dip a little. On the other hand, if it looks like the option period is about to end but property prices are on the rise, I might propose to you that we *extend* the option period for a short time to take advantage of this market trend. Of course we can only do this by mutual agreement.

These are just a few of the most common questions I've heard over the years. In reality, a seller could ask you anything, there are many different objections that can arise. What is key is that you listen to your seller's needs and fully understand their circumstances. Keep the focus on them rather than on your own needs. That is how you get to a win-win solution!

Remember to **fit the strategy to the situation**. The biggest "rookie mistake" I've seen people make is to suggest a strategy that is not suitable for a particular seller's circumstances, just because the investor is desperate for a deal. If you do this you will fail.

In general, my advice is: **always be honest!** Build up a rapport with your seller; build trust. This counts for more than anything. You are nothing without your integrity. Be up front, always work with integrity. *Work* with the seller; be on their side.

Later in the book we will go through a more extensive list of objections and discuss the process for dealing with them.

My First Lease-Option Deals

The first time I ever offered a lease-option deal was around 2006. I had been contacted by a seller in Aylesbury, near Milton Keynes, who had a property on the market for £350,000 and, as it wasn't too far from where I was living at the time, I went to see it. It was a five-bedroom house spread over three floors. It was a good property and I was keen to do a deal. However, the seller wasn't prepared to give me the discount I needed to make the BMV deal viable. Her situation was that she was going through a divorce and desperately needed a sale to get the equity out of the property. She just needed some cash to set up on her own.

I had been researching lease-options deals around this time, looking at how they had been used in commercial property deals and wondering if I could use the same structure in a residential property deal. I knew this deal wasn't the ideal scenario, that it wasn't the best fit for a lease-option deal. To be honest, I simply wanted to have a go at pitching my newfound baby to a seller. As I was leaving the property, having not been able to come to an agreement, I just threw it out there as a possibility. To be honest, I made a real hash of it! I was nervous because I wanted the property so badly, and I still wasn't 100% sure how lease-option deals worked and felt highly stressed by the whole situation. I started talking about how I could take over her mortgage with an option period to buy it. I was completely tongue-tied. I'm not even sure I explained clearly who would be granting whom an option! I'll never forget the look on her face as she stood there, holding the door open and calmly said, "Goodbye, Mr Wong". I left with my tail firmly between my legs.

But it didn't put me off. I kept doing my research and practising my pitch. I was sure there was a useful application of lease-option deals in residential property deals. And, finally, I was rewarded!

Not long after I crashed and burnt with the Aylesbury woman, I went to see a property in Nottingham. The male owner had contacted me and once I heard his story, I could tell that his particular circumstances were crying out for a lease-option deal. I was absolutely certain it was the best win-win scenario for both of us. I pitched it to him (perhaps with a little more confidence than I'd done in Aylesbury) and to my surprise he totally got it and agreed immediately. I was in! However, he then said, "So, what do we do next?" I was embarrassed to admit I didn't actually know!

Of course I quickly figured out the practical procedures for setting up the lease-option deal and since then I have never looked back; that first deal formed the basis of all the experience and knowledge I have gleaned since. I have probably negotiated well over 100 lease-option deals over the years I've been in business. About half of those were for myself and half were for other investors.

WIIFT

Remember the all-important golden rule when it comes to pitching lease-option deals to sellers ... always tell them **WIIFT (What's In It For Them)**!

As I've demonstrated, you don't go in straight off the bat saying, "Let me tell you why a lease-option deal would work here". They've never heard of the term "lease-option deal", so you'll only alienate them and make them cautious. Get away from the technical terms and tailor your pitch to show the seller what you can offer them and how you can take care of their needs: show them **what's in it for them**. This is why you *must* know your seller's circumstances inside out. What is specifically causing them pain? Is it an inability to make the mortgage payments that is causing them unbearable stress? If so, you tell them about how you can help them. If their "pain" is their tenancy problems – perhaps they have difficult tenants or are just struggling with the property maintenance, maybe because they became an "accidental landlord" – you lead with how you could help relieve that burden. In general, you get them talking about *their* PAIN and *their* NEEDS and then *you* offer SOLUTIONS. In most cases, you shouldn't even mention the terminology "lease-option deal" until you've been talking to them for a good while and have gained their trust.

At the end of the day, most sellers have only ever had experience of estate agents and prospective buyers coming to them with their own agendas, they are not used to someone saying: "Hey, what are your needs and how can I help you so that it's a win-win situation for both of us?"

Since my first lease-option deal, I have done countless more. It is now a tool I regularly use in the right situation. It is still an uncommon buying strategy in the world of residential property, and I am regarded as one of the world's foremost experts in lease-option deals for residential property. I regularly talk to authorities on the topic and also give seminars. I teach people how to do lease-option deals all over the world, including the UK, the Netherlands, Singapore, Malaysia, Australia and New Zealand.

Rent-To-Buy

In the way that lease-option deals are primarily driven by the *seller's* circumstances, this strategy – **Rent-To-Buy** – is driven primarily by the *buyer's* circumstances. There will be occasions when a rent-to-buy deal is seller-circumstance led, for example if the seller has a rundown property and wants to offer the tenant a rent-to-buy option where the buyer (tenant) takes on the responsibility for doing up the property; but this is moving into the next strategy, which I call "Bob The Builder".

Let's say that you want to become a homeowner, but you really don't have a single friend or family member to go to who could do a tenancy-in-common deal with you or act as your mortgage host. Well, there is another way. Whether you are currently renting and are interested in buying the property you live in or you are about to start renting (after perhaps living at home with your parents), there is a way that you can turn you situation into one that allows you to get onto the property ladder.

The Renter's Trap

As I've explained several times already, the Assured Shorthold Tenancy agreement that was introduced in the Housing Act 1980 really destroyed the rights of tenants. In most other big cities in the Western world, tenants have far more rights. In New York, Amsterdam and Paris, for example, once you have a tenancy, as long as you keep paying your rent, you can basically stay there as long as you like. It's quite difficult for the landlord to evict you! But for British tenants the landlord can usually evict you with two months notice. This is especially stressful if you are in a permanent job, if you have children in schools, and if you've made significant ties to an area. Also, when you have a long lease on a place, you can invest in making it your own. But when you are on an Assured Shorthold Tenancy agreement, you live for most of your life knowing that the landlord could throw you out with two month's notice so it's hard to get enthusiastic about taking care of the place!

As well as feeling insecure in your own home, as a renter in the UK you watch your money disappear every month with the knowledge that, no matter what happens, you will never benefit from the capital appreciation of the property. Plus, the landlord will only ever keep the property in adequate condition; they are unlikely to make any improvements while you are there and paying rent. And there's no point in *you* making any nice improvements because you will never benefit from the added value to the property.

With all that rent going "down the drain" there's not much hope of you saving for a deposit on your own place. We've already crunched the figures on this one and have seen that it's virtually impossible for a young person to save for a deposit and get a mortgage with the disparity between salaries and house prices these days.

Being a renter in Britain can feel exceptionally depressing at times! So ... how can we change this situation so that it is a win-win result for everyone? Well, let's ask a couple of questions about what everyone *wants*.

Question: What does the owner of the property want? Answer: A steady income stream and a capital gain in the long term.

Question: What does the renter (would-be homeowner) want? Answer: Security and autonomy in their own home, and the ability to benefit from the appreciation of the property, both through capital appreciation and by potentially adding value.

If the owner rents to the renter (would-be homeowner) in the conventional way, he gets *his* needs met. If the would-be homeowner was able to get a deposit together and qualify for a mortgage, he would get *his* needs met. *But ...* there is a way that **both parties can get their needs met** !

All About Control

Remember, as we've touched on before, the basic fact that most people miss is that having a mortgage does not mean you really own the property, it just means that you have **control** of the property. The point of having a mortgage is to get the benefits of a), b) and c) as mentioned above: to have security, independence and benefit from the capital appreciation of the property. When you have a mortgage, the bank or building society still technically owns the property; it just allows you to have complete control over it (unless you stop paying the mortgage, in which case they will eventually take it back).

So many people have this misconception when it comes to home "ownership" ... they confuse ownership with control. When you have a mortgage, you don't own the property, you just have the right to do what you want to the property, the right to stay in the property (as long as you keep paying the mortgage) and the ability to benefit from the capital appreciation of the property. It is the **terms and conditions** of your mortgage that give you these rights. So, what if you could change the **terms and conditions** of your tenancy agreement, whereby you are granted the no-obligation right to buy your property? You would then have the **same benefits as a mortgage holder**, i.e. the ability to benefit from the capital appreciation of the property and the right to stay in it for as long as you pay your rent until the day you exercise your option to buy.

A certain type of open-minded landlord, in a certain situation, may well be open to negotiating a less unconventional agreement that benefits you as well as them. As long as you have a good relationship with your landlord (or potential landlord), there is nothing to stop you from approaching the subject. You can start by asking him or her if they'd like to get a little more rent from you each month … that should make them sit up and listen!

What you would explain is that, although you are a renter at this point in time, your objective is to get on the property ladder. You would make the landlord an offer, the price that you would buy the property for in several years time. You'd ask him to give you an option agreement giving you the right (but crucially no obligation) to buy the property at that price for a certain length of time. Obviously, during this time you will have the right to remain in the property as long as you are paying your rent without the threat of eviction. You will ask the landlord for his blanket permission to do whatever you like to the property (because, of course, it is now in your interest to keep the property looking as nice as possible).

For all of this, you will pay your landlord a fee against the final purchase price of the property and a premium rent (a portion of which will also count against the final purchase price of the property).

Of course this is not an Assured Shorthold Tenancy agreement, this is a bespoke agreement, the **terms** of which you will have negotiated with the landlord. You would obviously have a qualified and experienced lawyer draw up this agreement.

You are now a tenant–buyer. You are paying a little more rent than you would otherwise, and you have paid a fee for the privilege, but for all that you control your property without having to be mortgage approved, you can stay in it for a considerable length of time, you can make whatever improvements you want to it and you will benefit from the capital appreciation. A nice position to be in!

So why wouldn't everyone do this? Because they don't know they can! It makes no financial sense to rent in in the UK in the conventional way, with no additional benefits. But a huge proportion of people in the UK are renting in the conventional way because they don't have a deposit and/or wouldn't qualify for a mortgage, and

don't know that there are other options available to them! Having said this, I always say to people, "it's simple but not easy, and don't rule it out until you try it".

Motivated Landlords

Would every landlord go for this kind of deal? Not necessarily. You have to find one in a situation where it looks a more attractive proposition to them than the alternative.

We've talked a little about motivated sellers (the only people you should deal with when making BMV deals and lease-option deals); now let's talk about motivated landlords.

In the same way that for every property for sale there is a seller with a *reason* for selling it ... for every property available for rent there is a landlord with a *reason* for renting it. Usually that landlord has chosen to get into the property business and wants to make a regular income from rental payments. We always tend to assume that the landlord is a professional landlord, someone who has chosen this path. However, sometimes a person becomes a landlord by accident. Some landlords are renting reluctantly. They might have inherited a property that needs a lot of updating that they can't afford to do. Or they might have had to relocate and were unable to sell the property at that time for whatever reason. Some landlords have found themselves in the position where the rent they receive is barely covering the mortgage that they have to pay out and would love a better solution.

It's also safe to say for *all* landlords that, while they like receiving rent, they don't necessarily like being responsible for the property!

If you want to know if a landlord is motivated, find out if they have any "pain". Perhaps your landlord has had bad tenants in the past. If so, he or she might be very receptive to the idea of excellent tenants with a strong incentive to take care of a property locked into a seven-year contract to stay in it. You could go to your landlord with a **solution** for the "pain" of bad tenants and the fear of future bad tenants. Perhaps your landlord really struggles with the responsibility for the property's maintenance, or can't charge enough rent to cover the mortgage. In this case, the **solution** you can offer is a premium on the rent and the taking over of the property maintenance in exchange for the deal you want (an option to buy the property in "x" number of years).

The bottom line is, not every landlord *wants* the benefit of being able to evict you with two months notice as part of an Assured Shorthold Tenancy agreement. Some would much rather give up that right in exchange for an agreement that benefits their personal situation more, they are just not offered this as a solution by a typical estate agent because it's not in the estate agent's interest to do themselves out of the negotiation fee that they can charge every year to renew the lease!

A landlord with any kind of pain is a *motivated* landlord.

Rent-To-Buy Deals In Practice

So what does a rent-to-buy deal look like in practice?

Let's say you're 32 years old. You've been renting in London for the past eight years, since moving out of home. You've graduated from living with friends to living on your own. You're on a salary of £30,000. You're paying rent of £1,000 for a studio flat in Streatham that you've lived in for two years. You love your flat. You wish you could own it. You like the area, it's convenient for your work and near your friends, but you know there's no way you could get together the deposit or qualify for the mortgage that would be needed to buy it because you've seen similar flats that are on the market for £200,000. You'd need a deposit of at least £20,000 (10%) if not more, and a salary of £60,000 to qualify for a £180,000 mortgage. You've got savings of £6,000.

You're not in a good position in terms of the conventional method of owning property.

This is what you could do. Approach your landlord with an offer. Ideally, work out where his or her "pain" might be coming from first. Perhaps they've inherited the property and struggle with the responsibility of maintenance. You also know your landlord is facing a few financial difficulties. Open the offer by pointing out that you've been an excellent tenant for the past two years. Then explain that you would be interested in taking on more responsibility for the property in exchange for extra security (presumably you are on a Assured Shorthold Tenancy agreement). Once you've got your landlord interested, explain that you would like to offer to pay the landlord an option fee of £3,000 against the purchase price, for the right to buy the property at today's price (£200,000) in seven years time. You offer to pay him an extra £200 a month in rent (a premium that, again, counts towards the purchase price), *plus* you say you will take on all the responsibility for the maintenance and improvement of the flat. What landlord isn't going to agree to that?

How is it a win-win? Well, you can see that the landlord gets an increased monthly payment, permanent tenants for seven years and an upfront fee. *You* get security, the ability to do what you want with the property, and the knowledge that you will have a property in your name in seven years time.

In seven years time, let's imagine the property has gone up to £260,000 and you decide to exercise your option. Your £200 per month amounts to £16,800 towards the purchase price, plus the initial fee of £3,000 and you now owe your landlord £180,200 (£200,000 less £19,800). So you need a mortgage of £180,200, but this is only around 70% of the value of the property. Most lenders will give you a mortgage over three times your salary if you have this much equity in the property. So even if your salary has only gone up to £48,000, you should be able to get your mortgage. If you can't, you'll flip the option to an investor and walk away with a profit of £79,800, which puts you in a much better position than you were in seven years ago. You've basically profited from a property as if you'd owned it. Or you have other options, such as mortgage hosting, or you could do a tenancy-in-common deal. Being in control of a property with at least £79,800 equity in it obviously puts you in a very strong negotiating position.

This is just one example of what could happen. Obviously every deal is bespoke. You might pay more premium rent if you don't have enough saved up for a fee. You might pay a larger fee but no share of the capital appreciation. Perhaps you make the option period five years, or ten years. The main thing to remember, as I keep saying, is that the *terms* of the deal are very much whatever you can make them! Just keep focused on WIIFT (what's in it for them) as you negotiate.

You could be an existing tenant approaching your landlord with this deal. You could be a prospective tenant offering a new potential landlord this deal. *Or* you could be a landlord seeking a tenant who would like to take advantage of this deal. A similar deal is common practice in the public sector where councils or housing associations do "shared ownership" schemes. Or a landlord might offer a rent-to-buy deal to a tenant under the specific conditions outlined in our next strategy …

"Bob The Builder"

This is really an application of the rent-to-buy strategy that is useful if you have a property that requires a considerable amount of work doing to it and you can find a tenant who is a builder. Basically, you would structure a rent-to-buy deal as described above, but rather than paying a large option fee and a premium on the rent, the builder/tenant agrees to do the necessary renovation work. This is a great deal for the builder because when builders typically quote for work, they put a considerable mark up on it to make a profit. When considering how much to reduce the option fee and premium by, you would factor in *this* quote. Say the quote was £20,000 for all the works, and the option fee and premium rent for the option period would come to £18,000 in total over six years. Well, you might take an option fee of £2,000 and no premium on the rent.

Of course, then the builder will do the work at a fraction of the price – in this case, say he manages to do the work for £8,000, it's like he's made a profit of £20,000.

Again, the seller/landlord gets a reliable tenant and doesn't have to pay up front for the work being done.

In 2007, I bought a property in Manchester. I learned the hard way that you should always do your due diligence. Although I sent someone to see the property, I didn't get enough detail from them and I never actually went to see it myself before completing the deal. It was during the big property boom (in fact, just before the big crash) and one of the few real mistakes I made. After completing the sale, I paid this property a visit. It was completely dilapidated! Everything, from the windows to the toilet, was broken. The kitchen was a disaster. The whole house needed to be refurbished. The valuation report had mentioned none of this. During these times it was quite common to see valuers inflate the price of properties, and also not to mention any cosmetic damage … and the banks were willing to lend on this basis. As the house itself was structurally sound, the valuer had not mentioned the terrible state it was in cosmetically. It was my responsibility for not doing thorough due diligence on the property, but I was truly in shock when I saw it!

The house was a terrace house in a not-so-nice part of Manchester. It was a typical two-up-two-down property, with a toilet on the ground floor, a frog-infested fishpond in the overgrown jungle of a garden and a mouldy bathroom full of damp. There was no central heating and every patch of wall needed repairing.

I had bought the property for around £70,000, but when I got the quote back from my builder it looked like I was going to have to spend another £18,000 on it to get it habitable! I had no choice. If I didn't do the work and kept it vacant, I'd lose money as I'd get no rent for it. So I asked my builder if he'd like to invest in the property in some way. He said he'd love to but he hadn't been able to get a mortgage because he was Polish and hadn't lived in the UK long enough. He also didn't have any savings for a deposit.

I explained the whole lease-option theory to him. I offered him a seven-year option to buy the property from me at £80,000. In exchange, he would do it up at his own cost. I told him that, as soon as the property was ready, we would rent it out and split the profit from the rent between us. I knew this would also incentivize him to get the work done as soon as possible.

To my surprise, he was extremely enthusiastic about it. He proposed doing up the whole property to quite a high standard, so putting in a new kitchen and bathroom and windows throughout the property, as well as installing central heating. Obviously, doing all the work himself, he didn't need to put a mark-up on it and probably got trade prices for all his materials. I would say he probably spent around £5,000 or so.

The work took six weeks in total and we got a tenant immediately. If we'd put the property straight back on the market it would have been worth around £90,000 and this guy had an option to buy it for £80,000, so on paper he was already £5,000 (£10,000 less the work spend) in profit! And, of course, if he'd exercised his option at that exact moment, buying it for £80,000, I would have made an instant £10,000 profit because I'd bought it for £70,000.

That's not a bad result on paper. Within six weeks of me completing on this property, I had a fully renovated property available in Manchester. I had £10,000 paper profit and my builder had around £5,000. Boom! Plus, I think we rented the property out for around £650 a month and the mortgage was £250. So we split the profit equally and we both got a passive monthly income of £200 each.

I went from having a liability to an asset. I just had to structure the deal creatively. This is a great example of what can happen when you think creatively … while everyone else is following the herd!

Part Now, Part Later

This very simple strategy does exactly what it says on the tin.

If you, as an investor, are looking for a 30% discount on a property worth £100,000, i.e. you want to buy it for £70,000 but the seller is sticking at wanting £80,000 for it, you can structure a deal where you agree to pay £70,000 today and £10,000 in the future. So you could offer the seller £70,000 today and £10,000 in seven years time. Obviously, in seven years the property is likely to be worth much more (perhaps £150,000), so you can easily take £10,000 of equity out of it to pay the original seller. This is simply a slight spin on a basic BMV deal if the seller won't budge on the price. It's another way of structuring it so that you both get what you want.

Other Strategies

There are three other strategies worth mentioning, although I didn't want to include them in my main strategies for the following reasons.

One is "Sale And Rent Back". I haven't included this as one of my main strategies because it is virtually impossible to do now, due to stringent legislation. The second is the "Sandwich Option", which I haven't included in my main strategies simply because I have not personally used this strategy to date, although I have heard on good authority that it can be very effective. The third strategy is "Seller As Lender". Again, I didn't include this in my main strategies because it is not one I've used myself. However, a very close business associate of mine pioneered it and I intend to use it as soon as the right situation arises!

Sale And Rent Back

This was a strategy that was once very popular and we did several such deals around 2006/07. "Sale And Rent Back" is basically a way of people releasing the equity in their property after they've paid off the mortgage. Say you've lived in your property for 25 years, but you're on the verge of retiring. It would be difficult to re-mortgage your property because you won't have a salary. This would also make it hard for you to get a decent-sized bank loan. You could sell up and downsize, but you might not want to move. A simple solution could be to sell your property to an investor and rent it back from him. The investor will obviously want to buy the property at BMV and then rent it back to the owner for a market rent. It's a great deal for the investor because there is no better tenant than someone who has lived in and loved a property for years.

Sadly, some so-called investors (but really unscrupulous people with no integrity!) got greedy and, after completing these sales, would turn around and *evict* the original owners and put the properties back on the market for a profit. The original homeowners would then be devastated at being unable to live in their own home (which is why they did the deal in the first place ... to carry on living in their home but benefit today from the equity in it.)

As a result, this practice of "sale and rent back" got a lot of very bad press and eventually caught the attention of the OFT (Office of Fair Trading) and FSA (Financial Standards Authority – which has now become the FCA, the Financial Conduct Authority). Legislation was put in place to protect homeowners from falling prey to this kind of behaviour. Nowadays, the criteria you must meet for doing this kind of deal are so stringent that most investors can't even qualify. It's a real shame because, when followed with integrity, it was always a great deal for both the *ethical* investor and the original homeowner.

Unfortunately it's often the case that a few bad eggs spoil things for the majority. This is why I put such a *huge* emphasis on **ETHICS** when I mentor my students. If you mess something up, you mess things up for *everyone!* I am actually extremely picky these days about who I will do business with. I have worked very hard to build and maintain a spotless reputation and I don't want anyone tainting it. I don't just sell leads to anyone, I am very careful about who I take leads to. I will only deal with people I know.

Sandwich Options

These should be easy to understand now that you understand lease-option deals and rent-to-buy. You could theoretically combine them and do what is known as a sandwich option deal. As I say, I have not used the strategy myself, but I do know of people using it in Australia and New Zealand. If you understand lease-options from the point of view of the investor, and you know how rent-to-buy works from the point of view of the tenant, you could do an immediate option with any "tenant–buyer", i.e. use a lease-option structure with someone who wants to get into a property. You don't have to wait until you have a highly-motivated seller or a dilapidated property for a "Bob the Builder" situation. You basically do a lease-option with a seller and immediately rent it out to a tenant–buyer under a "rent-to-buy" deal so that they have an option to buy from you (for the same period you have the option to buy from the seller) at a higher price. When the tenant exercises their option to buy, you exercise *your* option to buy and the difference is your profit.

Seller As Lender

In this scenario, the seller would literally become an independent lender. This is an ingenious and unconventional way of buying and earning money from property.

At the time of writing, my close business associate in Holland is in the process of negotiating a deal just like this. She was contacted by a couple who had inherited a property worth around €200,000 that had no mortgage on it. They wanted advice on the best way to make money from it. They knew that to sell the property and put a lump sum in the bank was not the best way forward because the bank will only ever give you a miniscule amount of interest. Their other option was to rent out the property themselves, but then they would become responsible for the maintenance and doing the property up (it was in need of some updating), and they really didn't feel they would have the time or desire to become landlords.

The deal that my associate is structuring for them is potentially a great win-win. Under the terms of the deal, the owners would transfer the title to my associate, the investor. She would officially become the owner of the property. However, to finance the purchase, my associate would effectively be *borrowing* the €200,000 (on paper) from the owner. Every month the owners will receive a repayment of interest plus some capital, exactly as if they were a mortgage lender!

My associate, an experienced landlady, plans to update the property and then rent it out for €900. Her monthly repayment (capital plus interest) to the original owners would be €500. So she would come away with €400 profit each month. Some of this will be kept aside for maintenance and to cover any vacant periods, but a good portion of it will be profit.

On paper, this doesn't look too different from the original couple simply renting the property out through an estate agent and receiving a profit each month less some maintenance costs and management fees. But in this scenario two independent parties can get a profit with no middleman making a cut! The seller would be *charging* a much higher rate of interest by lending the money than they would collect by having the money in the bank. We get what is effectively the equivalent of a 100% mortgage (that you could never get from a bank). This is a win-win. The couple get a good monthly income with absolutely no responsibilities. The investor owns a property and gets a rental income without having to arrange a mortgage or put down a deposit. The investor obviously has to guarantee the seller a monthly payment, just as she would have to guarantee paying a traditional mortgage lender. The original owner obviously has repossession rights if the tenants don't pay the rent, just like a traditional lender. (Incidentally, "don't try this one at home". You should be a very experienced investor with a highly-experienced lawyer by your side before you try it!)

*   *   *

Hopefully you can see now that the minute you open your mind, you will find so many strategies available to you. There are so many ways in which you can own/control – and profit from – property. I've highlighted seven strategies that I've used, but there are countless strategies you could use. I hope you invent one and make it work. Please come and share it with me if you do!

At the end of the day, in the real world, it is unlikely that you will get to apply these strategies in a linear, black-and-white way. You don't go into a deal with a strategy in mind. They are for troubleshooting problems. I am merely giving you a box of tools.

In the final section of this book, we will be going through several case studies to show how some of the main strategies described in this section can work in practice. But I will show you how you don't just pick a strategy and apply it, you often go to your toolbox and see what you might be able to use when the going gets tough. You always hope to get that straightforward BMV deal, but life rarely works out like that. When you hit the inevitable bumps in the road, you need your toolbox of strategies to pick from to see if you can find a way to help the deal along.

In the case studies I describe, for instance, you will see how a couple of BMV deals that looked straightforward on paper eventually turned into lease-option deals. You will learn about an extraordinary case in which we ended up having to negotiate with the authorities in a foreign country! You will see how no property deal is ever straightforward. You can never predict the twists and turns you might encounter but, armed with a few possible alternative strategies, you've got a better chance of completing a deal than if you stick to what people traditionally try to do. Negotiating your way through a complex deal is challenging, but it's all part and parcel of the fun. Remember: the sweetest victories are the hardest won!

I am sure you will be intrigued and amazed to read some of the stories my associates and I have heard in our years in business. Often there are heightened emotions at play and all manner of dramatic events taking place!

9

Dealing With Objections

So far, you have learnt that to be successful in today's property market, you need to become a property *entrepreneur* and that as an entrepreneur, you must treat your involvement in the property market as a *property business*. You also hopefully understand a successful business has to be *systemized* and you know how you can build a *successful value system*. You are also now informed of the *specific strategies* that will enable you to make new types of property deals as a new style of dealmaker. So the final piece of the puzzle is how to *put this into practice*. And when you do that, you have to deal with *real people*. And this is the point at which all the theory in the world can't help you ... because people have objections to anything new!

Whenever you are proposing something new to someone, something they have not heard of before, you will be faced with a barrage of objections. You need to know how to handle these objections.

I am going to summarize some of the most common objections I hear and describe how I deal with them.

When you start talking to sellers about buying and selling houses in a non-traditional way, i.e. without an estate agent involved and by way of a deal that is more about the terms than the price, you will obviously face objections. So how do you deal with these?

Well, the most important thing to remember is *never fight an objection*. You don't fight fire with fire. You should readily expect objections, so don't be taken aback. You need to have your answers to the most common objections prepared. Your communication should be shaped by being in the right frame of mind to deal with objections. Start your negotiations expecting the answer to be "no" and work on getting to a "yes". Most people give up the moment they hear "no". If you expect it, you'll be ready for it.

In Stephen R. Covey's book, *The 7 Habits of Highly Effective People*, he advocates that you should seek to understand first, before you seek to be understood. If empathy is your first port of call, you immediately put yourself in the most persuasive position. Once you show someone that you understand their point of view, that you fully appreciate their perspective, they will trust you and listen to you.

I teach my students to remember the words **FEEL**, **FELT** and **FOUND**. As in: "I know how you *feel* about *x* because in the past others have *felt* that way, but what we have *found* is that in reality ... etc."

When you say this, you immediately display a high degree of empathy. You are showing that you can stand in their shoes and see the situation from their point of view. By telling them that others have felt the same way, you are ensuring that they do not feel like they are the exception, that it's not a unique problem. Then, when you offer them the solution, explaining what you've found in practice, they are going to listen to you *because* you have empathized with them and you've reassured them that they are not alone.

The key rules to follow, when faced with seller's objections are:

1. Don't create a conflict.

2. Don't get angry.

3. Don't get defensive.

Remember: when you get angry and defensive, people automatically assume that you are guilty of the very thing they are worried about.

So now let's go through some of the common objections that people have to BMV deals.

Objection No. 1: "You're asking for too big a discount; you're being greedy."
When I hear this objection, I generally say, "I understand where you're coming from. I know how you *feel*. I've heard other people say this in the past; other people have *felt* the same way as you. In reality, however, what I've *found* is that, if a seller's profit is more important than the speed of the sale, then perhaps a cash-buyer solution – one where the investor makes a greater profit in exchange for a quick sale – is probably not for you. It's the nature

of the business that cash-buyers will require a discount, otherwise they cannot operate. This is how we operate. I can also assure you that we are being up front about the exact level of discount we will require, and we will not ask for a greater discount down the line, which is how some cash-buyers operate."

Objection No. 2: "I've heard of other cash investors who only require a 5% discount, why are you asking for 20%?"
Again, I start with saying, "I understand where you're coming from. I know how you feel. I know other people have felt the same way as you in the past." I then explain: "In reality, however, what I've found is that those other cash investors will keep chipping away at the price. They may say they only want a 5% discount at the beginning, but by the time you are about to complete they will insist on a further discount and basically hold you to ransom, refusing to complete unless you give them the discount they want. They hook you in with the promise of 5% and then change it. As I've explained, all professional cash investors need to buy properties at a discount, that's how they stay in business, they require profits. However, when I agree to a certain percentage discount, I don't try to change it. I've been in the industry a long time and I know that 5% is not a realistic figure to sustain a business on. I can sometimes lower my percentage from 20%, but then I might negotiate slightly different terms to balance the deal. The point is, whatever offer we agree on, I will stick to it and not try to renegotiate at a critical point – a practice I view as blackmail and deeply unethical. Of course you also have to remember that my offer is based on the valuation – it's a fixed percentage of a yet-to-be-confirmed valuation. There is always a chance that the valuation will come back lower than we expected, in which case the *price* will naturally drop, but the percentage is still the same. It is part of my strict code of ethics that I will always be up front at the point of making the deal and give my final offer. There are no hidden costs and I will never try to renegotiate arbitrarily. My business is completely transparent.

Objection No. 3: "Our deal is based on a presumed valuation of my property, how do I know you will honour the deal if the valuation comes back lower than we expected?"
To this objection I say: "I understand exactly how you feel and you are not alone, others have felt like this in the past. However,

in reality, what we've found is that it helps people to think of the deal in terms of the percentage below the valuation rather than get attached to a fixed figure, because, yes, there is always the possibility that the valuation comes back lower than expected. We use exactly the same tools as the surveyor, so our valuation *should* be pretty close, but there is always the possibility of something unforeseen coming up. I once had a buyer who did not disclose that her property had been in an auction. We made the initial offer, which was a percentage below our basic valuation. However, when we did our due diligence we discovered that the property had been in an auction and had not made its reserve. Few people understand that this creates a kind of permanent mark against the property, in that it affects the valuation. Because this seller's property had been in an auction, the valuation came back much lower than expected, which, after the percentage discount we had agreed on, was not a price she could accept as it didn't even cover what she owed on the mortgage. She could have accepted it (our offer was still on the table) and owed the lender the balance, but she chose not to. Understanding that the offer is specifically 'a percentage below the official valuation figure' will help you to avoid disappointment. Hopefully, the valuation comes back as expected or (on the very odd occasion) even more, but you should manage your expectations by keeping the percentage and *not a fixed figure* in your mind. The example given above, of the woman whose property was down-valued after not making its reserve in an auction, is also a good example of the fact that the seller *always* has the choice, is always in control. She could have chosen to sell to us, but she chose not to. I constantly remind sellers that they are *in control*, that *it is their choice* whether to sell to me or not."

Objection No. 4: "I'm worried that there may be hidden costs."
When I hear this objection, again I start with, "I understand exactly how you feel and you are not alone, others have been worried and have felt like this in the past. However, in reality, you can be reassured that there will *never* be any hidden costs when you are dealing with my company, from me or any of my associates, or anyone working under my franchise (Network Property Buyers). I can't speak for other cash investors, but I can assure you that I have a code of conduct that everyone associated

with my company must adhere to. If they do not, their license to do business under my company name is revoked. My business is completely transparent. It's really very simple. I make you an offer, a fixed percentage below the official valuation of your property. We agree on a period of time during which I have the exclusive right to buy your property and then *I* start spending *my* money on getting the deal to go through. I commission the valuation, I hire the lawyers (including your lawyer if you cannot afford to pay your legal fees) and we proceed with the purchase. At any time you have the right to back out. If you do, I have lost the money I have already spent on the deal, but you have lost nothing. I know there are some unethical companies out there who try to make money from people in desperate situations. I've heard of companies that charge potential sellers an upfront fee for a valuation in order to lock in the seller and virtually hold them to ransom. I do not believe in trying to make money out of sellers up front like that! That is not a practice that will be conducted by me or by anyone working under my company name."

Objection No. 5: "You told me that you can complete in four weeks, so why do you want a three-month option?"
Once more, I use the "feel–felt–found" guidelines to deal with this objection. I say, "Yes, I understand exactly how you feel and you are not alone, others have felt concerned and unsure about this in the past. However, in reality what we've found is that, while we do everything in our power to ensure that the sale goes through in four weeks, there are often things that crop up that are outside our control. Searches can be delayed or come back with issues that need to be resolved; leaseholder enquiries can be notoriously laborious; all sorts of things can happen when conveyancing begins, and we have to allow for that. In fact, this is one of the reasons we use the same, trusted lawyers time and time again, and also why we suggest that sellers use lawyers recommended by us rather than their family lawyers, because we know we can trust these law firms to act as quickly and efficiently as possible. Our lawyers are fast, honest and reliable. We even cover the seller's legal fees to ensure that there are no potential hold ups. We don't want delays any more than the seller does! Our goal is always to complete in the four weeks, as quickly as possible, but we have to cover ourselves."

As I've explained before, we need that three-month exclusivity window to insure us against any unforeseen delays. The buyer needs to be protected too, especially when the buyer is investing their own money in the legal fees and valuation. Without an exclusivity period there is nothing to stop the seller going elsewhere and leaving the buyer with out-of-pocket expenses that have to be covered. I've had experiences where sellers seem to drop off the face of the earth and become completely uncontactable. In those circumstances I simply have to write off any expenses I've incurred. In many instances, though, the seller comes back six months later, with their tail between their legs, explaining that they'd gone elsewhere, with another buyer they believed was giving them a better deal, but that the deal had fallen through and they want to come back to me! Often they've been wooed by what they thought was a better offer, only to find out that the other buyer was a charlatan who tried to hit them with hidden charges and then insisted the price be dropped at the eleventh hour. (Unfortunately this business, like many others, does attract some unethical people.) When the seller comes back to us they are usually more desperate than ever, but I have to explain that I can't necessarily offer the same deal.

Objection No. 6: "If you pay my legal fees, is it not a conflict of interests? Doesn't this mean that the lawyer is representing you and not me?"
This is quite an easy objection to deal with. I still start by saying, "I understand exactly how you feel and you are not alone, others have been worried and have felt like this in the past. However, in reality, you can be reassured that all our lawyers are governed by The Law Society and thus *must* act in the interest of the client with whom they make an agreement. When a lawyer agrees to represent *you*, they represent *you*, regardless of who pays the fees. You must have heard of court cases where the side that loses is ordered to pay the legal costs. That shows you how it is immaterial who pays the bill … lawyers have to represent their client's best interests, if they didn't they would be in huge trouble with The Law Society and would risk losing their license. (Of course, having said this, if you want to pay your own legal fees … I'm more than happy for you to do that! I only offer to pay because the seller is usually having financial difficulties and I want to ensure

that they don't incur extra costs. I want the deal to go through as quickly as possible because we both stand to gain from it.)"

Objection No. 7: "You say you want to help me. How do I know you are genuine? That you're not trying to fool me?"
As usual, I start with my opening of, "I appreciate how you feel and I've heard others before you say that they've felt the same …" I then go on to explain: "I am a businessman; I am not a charity worker. I make no secret of the fact that I am also helping my business by helping you. Yes, I want to help you move on with your life, but you should never forget that I am doing what is good for my business, too. I'm always looking for a win-win. In my opinion a win-lose doesn't work because good business should always be about exchange of value. I get something that's valuable to me (a profit) and you get something that is valuable to you (release from debt). When you buy a mobile phone, it's always a win-win. The company who sold it to you gets something valuable (a profit) and you get something of value (a phone that enhances your life). If you visit a restaurant and the food is terrible, the restaurant gets its profit but you do not get any value, it's a win-lose. In my opinion, that is not good business! How long do you think that restaurant is going to stay in business if its customers are all unhappy with the food? Eventually any win-lose situation becomes a lose-lose situation. If value is not exchanged on both sides, it's not a good business arrangement."

My business has been thriving since 2005, that's ten years (at time of writing). If I hadn't maintained win-win arrangements, I wouldn't have stayed in business so long. My company is one of the longest established home-buying companies of its kind. At this point I've streamlined the process, I've ironed out all the kinks, I have a watertight formula that gives the best value to both my company and to the seller.

Objection No. 8: "You're the person I've been dealing with, but now you're telling me it's not your actual cash that's buying my property. Why aren't I dealing with the guy with the cash?"
Once more, I begin by saying, "I understand how you feel and I know other people in your situation have felt the same way in the past …". And then I explain how my company works. I say, "Obviously I can't physically buy every property I am offered

myself. My company literally deals with hundreds of enquiries every month. Some I buy, some I offer to other investors in my group. I have a pool of thoroughly vetted and trusted investors who want to put their money in property but want to use my expertise to find and negotiate the deals. However, what I *do* offer is my guarantee that the deal will go through. When the property is being bought with another investor's cash, if for any reason there is a problem, I guarantee that I will buy it myself. I effectively underwrite every sale. If I make the offer and we agree on a deal, then you have my guarantee that it will happen, no matter whose money buys the property in the end."

Objection No. 9: "What if I don't have enough equity in my property to give you the discount that you need?"
I often hear this concern, and after reassuring the investor that I understand exactly how they feel and that they are not alone because others have been similarly worried and have felt like this in the past, I explain that I will always be honest. I will say something like: "The fact is, I do need to make a profit so if there is not enough equity in the property for you to accept my offer without still owing too much money yourself, then the deal can't be done and I will be up front about that. However, while other companies might say, 'I can't help you then' and walk away, I will always try to find a solution. If I can figure out a constructive way of helping you while making enough profit myself to justify doing the deal, I'll do it. Sometimes this means making a deal where the property actually stays in your name but we take control of it and pay the mortgage based on an agreement that makes us the legal owners at a later fixed date for a fixed price." (This will pave the way for me to explain how a lease-option deal works.) "Again, no matter what, I am always looking to make a deal that is win-win. If it's not a win-win, we won't do the deal, simple as that. In some cases we just have to get a little creative to ensure that everyone wins!"

Objection No. 10: "I've spoken to my regular family lawyer and he's advising me not to go into this deal with you."
When I hear this objection, after I've reassured the seller that I understand how he or she feels and that others have felt the same in the past, I go on to explain that the only reason for a

lawyer's objection is that they are unfamiliar with this type of deal. "In reality it is actually unprofessional and unethical for your lawyer to advise you against a deal that is in your best interests just because they have not experienced the deal structure before. They are letting their personal feelings, fear and inexperience dictate your future. The deal is legal and ethical, if unconventional. I have done countless deals and have expert lawyers who negotiate them. I am always happy for your family lawyer to speak with *my* lawyer to help him or her understand how the deal works and to reassure them that it is all legal and ethical. It is understandable that they feel unsure about the deal if they haven't worked on something like it before, but this is not a reason to tell you *not* to do it, it is actually a great opportunity for them to expand their horizons, learn something new and help you in the process!"

10

The Seven Golden Rules For Property Entrepreneurs

Finally, I want to share with you my *Seven Golden Rules* for property entrepreneurs. If you've absorbed all the information you've read so far in this book, these will be fairly obvious, but it's still worth clearly identifying them. I recommend writing them down so you can refer to them, easily and often, as you build your property business. I still follow them today. Every time I'm involved in a deal, I check I'm following my own Golden Rules. I know that if I've followed all of them, I have the best chance of making a profitable deal.

The Golden Rules are:

1. Always deal **directly** with **motivated** sellers.

2. Remember to negotiate **terms** as well as price.

3. Only ever make a **win-win** deal.

4. Ensure all your deals are **ethical**.

5. Keep playing the **numbers game**.

6. Put as **little money down** as possible.

7. Adopt an **entrepreneurial mindset**.

Always Deal *Directly* With *Motivated* Sellers

Remember, *motivated* sellers think and behave differently from other sellers. Similarly, *entrepreneurial* property investors should think and behave differently from other property investors.

When a seller is motivated, it means that they have bigger priorities than making a profit on their property. They may need instant cash, or they may need to be free of their obligations quickly, or they may need to avoid having their property repossessed. Whatever their reason, *their* need is not profit motivated. If you can give them what they need, you can maximize your profit, which – as an entrepreneurial businessperson – is *your* motivating force.

You can quite easily see that it would not help either party to have a middleman, with yet another "need", involved! Thus you must only ever deal **directly** with **motivated** sellers.

Negotiate *Terms* In Addition To Price

Agreeing the price is only one part of a complete deal. The *terms* of the deal are paramount.

The main difference between the strategies I've laid out for property entrepreneurs, and the conventional way of investing in property, is that each deal done using one of these strategies is unique. When you invest in the traditional way, the contract – containing the *terms* of your deal – will look, more or less, like every other contract that every other investor has used. The only thing that really changes, from deal to deal, is the price.

When you are structuring a deal using one of these unconventional strategies, you **MUST** remember that you start with a more or less blank slate, and it is up to you to **negotiate the terms of the deal**. Obviously you go in with a loose structure in your head, but what you come out with may look nothing like what you were aiming for.

You have to be an absolute expert at negotiating before you go in and introduce ideas to a potential seller (or buyer) that they have never been exposed to before. There is huge scope for people misunderstanding you and walking away from the deal. If you try this as an inexperienced property entrepreneur, you could burn many bridges. Ensure that you *learn* from someone experienced at doing these deals. Hone your negotiating skills. Most people think they are much better negotiators than they are in practice. There is a huge difference between understanding the *theory* of good negotiating skills and actually putting them into *practice*!

Only Make A *Win-Win* Deal

The ethos of every strategy in this book challenges the false belief that in every deal there is a winner and a loser. I have demonstrated, again and again, that it is possible to ensure two winners in every deal. If you start by setting out firstly what you ultimately want, and then look at WIIFT (what's in it for them), you will be able to keep your deal win-win. Remember, the "win" for the seller is often just the fact that they get to walk away from a property that they can no longer afford to pay the mortgage on.

Ensure Your Deals Are *Ethical*

Your reputation is one of your most important assets and you must protect it religiously. Once you damage your reputation, it is very hard to repair it again. All your deals *must* be ethical. Property investors *per se* have not always had the best reputation so you are fighting an uphill battle from the get go. Ensure you do everything possible to keep your practices and your deals squeaky clean.

Also remember that you are a niche part of a huge industry, so everything you do will impact on the other people in that niche. The example I gave of "sale and rent back" deals that were abused by unethical investors is the perfect example of how some unscrupulous people can ruin things for everyone else. Those deals worked very well for both investors and homeowners. Many people benefited from them. Now, just because a few people got greedy, very few people can benefit from this strategy.

Always Play The *Numbers Game*

Remember the 100-10-5-3-1 rule. For every deal you aim to complete, you need to be analysing 100 potential deals. Some of these will be leads that come through your marketing machine; some will come through other channels, such as a property network or auctions. You want to do five deals a year? You need to be analysing 500 a year. For 10 deals, analyse 1,000 and so on. You set the goal, you choose your target, but then it's about reverse engineering it back to what you need to do at the start of the process in order to have the best chance of meeting those targets, of achieving those goals. Of course, this rule is only a guideline. You may hit the jackpot with the very first sellers you speak to. One of my students from a few years ago, who I taught lead generation to, went out and started to generate leads and the first two people she spoke to turned into deals.

Put As *Little Money Down* As Possible

Never forget the principle of leverage. The less money you have tied up in a property, the more leveraged your investment is, i.e. the greater the return on your investment. Always keep as little of your capital tied up as possible because the more liquid capital you have to play with, the more leveraged investments you can make. Keep your money working for you. When it's tied up as equity, it's not working for you. Of course, you need to stay aware of the dangers of negative equity in a volatile market, but when you're doing BMV deals, you're somewhat protected against this. Plus, as long as you don't need to sell the property, as long as you are **cash positive** (i.e. your rental income covers the mortgage and provides you with some profit) then you're fine. As long as you can sit on the property while it is in negative equity, you can ride out the storm. Prices will eventually go up again and you'll get back into positive equity.

Adopt An *Entrepreneurial Mindset*

Earlier in the book, I went through the qualities of an entrepreneur. Those qualities will always help you when you are making deals and building your business. Remember: being entrepreneurial is all about being **creative** and **learning new strategies**. Entrepreneurs jump off cliffs and build their aeroplanes on the way down. No matter how often I say to people, "the property business is *simple* but not *easy*" and warn them that it will take a huge amount of hard work and adaptability, they still complain when the going gets tough. Keep that entrepreneurial mindset and you will accept pitfalls when you come across them, knowing that being an entrepreneur is all about finding a way to dig yourself out of holes! Again … this is not a business for the faint-hearted.

*   *   *

Maybe you are not going to build your own property business, maybe you are going to invest in a property fund. Even if you do that, you should ensure that the fund you choose adheres to these Golden Rules. Otherwise, how do you know that your money is being invested wisely? A lot of people lose money when they invest in property funds because they are lazy; they don't do their due diligence to find out exactly how the fund invests their money. Investing in a property fund is a great idea, as long as the fund is being run and operated in the most efficient and profitable way.

You have to do your research; most people don't. Most people just think to themselves: "Property is a great investment, everyone knows that, I want to put my money in property but I don't want to do the work of finding and buying properties, so I'll just put my money into a property fund and let someone else do the work." People do this with their savings and pension funds, too. Why would you trust someone else to make money for *you*? Most people are in the investment game to make money for *themselves.* Just think of the fortunes people lost by giving their money to Bernie Madoff! They simply didn't do enough research or ask enough questions.

If you don't do the right research and you put your money in someone else's hands, you are just gambling.

I believe that, if you build a property business with an efficient system and you follow these Golden Rules, then you have the best chance of becoming a successful property entrepreneur. It won't happen overnight. You must be patient. Follow my other Golden Rule for life … never, never, never give up!

Of course, as with any skill, you can learn all the theory you like but it will always be a whole new ball game when you come to put your knowledge into practice. If you are new to property investing, you should *definitely* find someone to shadow and learn from. Go to courses, read more books, get educated and get practical experience alongside someone who's been doing it longer than you.

Ultimately, give your business the best possible chance!

With all that in mind, as promised, I'm now going to share with you some of my real-life experiences of being a property entrepreneur. I'm going to show you this new approach to dealmaking in practice. These are some of my best learning experiences … the good, the bad and the ugly!

All the deals – the case studies – in the following chapters were either made by my company or by my close associates with my involvement. You will see how every case is unique because of the seller's situation.

PART

III

THE REAL DEAL

CHAPTER 11

Probate Property In Leeds

In late 2014, we were contacted by a man who had inherited a three-bedroom semi-detached house in Leeds. He had actually been living in the property for many years. It belonged to his late mother and she had left it to him when she had died earlier that year. The house was in terrible state of repair; the whole property needed a refurbishment, from top to bottom. This man was under the impression that the house was worth £80,000. This was based on the fact that his neighbour in the same street had sold an identical house a few months back, around June 2014. He wanted the money as soon as possible in order to pay off some debts. He also wanted to relocate; he didn't want to live there anymore. He needed a quick sale.

An interesting factor in this story is that this man found out about us because he met a woman who was refurbishing a property in the same street as him. She was actually one of our students. He approached her and asked if she was a property investor looking for investment properties in the area. She said she wasn't looking for any more properties herself, but put him in touch with us.

My negotiator had a chat with this seller over the phone and she explained to him that we could certainly arrange a quick sale, but it would be on condition that we bought the property at 30% below market value. If the valuation did indeed come back at £80,000, that would mean we would purchase at £55,000. With the guarantee that he would get that cash out of the property within three months, the seller was happy with the offer.

With a deal on the table, our next job was to do our due diligence on the property. That began with looking at the seller's property in comparison with the neighbouring property that had sold for £80,000.

What we saw, unfortunately, gave us pause. The photos of the neighbouring house that had sold for £80,000 showed a completely refurbished property in excellent condition. By comparison, the photographs of our seller's place showed the house to be in a very sorry state. There were metal bars across all the windows, which made it look particularly unwelcoming, the inside was full of clutter and was in a state of disrepair throughout, and it was clear no one had updated or even thoroughly cleaned the property in years. We could see all the potential as the house was spacious and full of character, but it needed plenty of work before it was comparable to the neighbouring house that had sold for £80,000 about six months before.

(I have to say, this was by no means the worst property I have ever seen. That accolade must go to a property I viewed in the High Wycombe area. I am still haunted to this day by the images and smells from that property. Every room was strewn with dirty clothes, junk and garbage. There was literally not a space of floor visible. The place was overrun with animals. There were cages filled with parrots and rodents. Cats and dogs roamed throughout the house and in every room there were piles of animal faeces. It was a hot day and all the windows were tightly shut so the smell was overpowering. I couldn't get out of the place fast enough and actually threw up in a bush outside. This was the kind of place where you thoroughly wiped your feet on the way *out* of the place!)

My negotiator told the seller in Leeds that his property did not compare to the one that had sold in his street. He was under the impression that the property only needed "a little cosmetic work", but it was quite clear to us that it needed a new kitchen, a new bathroom, new flooring and new wall coverings, and that was before we had even looked at the potential for it needing any structural work.

The problem, sometimes, is that people who have lived with their property in a certain condition get used to that standard, they don't have an appreciation of what is expected of a pristine property.

We told the seller that, given what we had discovered, we felt the house needed around £10,000–15,000 worth of work doing to it, putting its value at around £65,000–70,000. With a 30% discount on the market value of the house, that meant that our offer would drop to £45,000–49,000. We were very clear with him, showing him photos of his property compared to the one that had sold for £80,000 and explaining what it would cost to bring his up to the same standard.

In the end we agreed on a fixed purchase price of £50,000 (which would still be a 23% discount for us if the valuation came back at the lower end of the scale, i.e. £65,000). We were realistic with him at every step of the process, as we didn't want to get his hopes up. Unless he was prepared to walk away with £50,000 there was no point in pursuing the matter any further.

Realizing that we were his best option, that he could wait months and months for an estate agent to find a buyer willing to take on the property, the seller agreed to our offer and we signed a three-month lock-out agreement with him. We explained that this was to safeguard us during the conveyancing process, to ensure we could not be gazumped by anyone. (Again, remember with straight BMV deals you are particularly vulnerable to being gazumped.)

If ever a seller challenges us over the lock-out agreement, we just explain that we have to have protection in exchange for the guaranteed, fast turnaround. The conveyancing process is expensive and we cannot start instructing solicitors and paying for searches if we are not given an exclusive period. In any case, as we always point out, even if the seller is tempted by a slightly higher offer from another buyer, there is no guarantee that such a buyer is genuine or will not ask for a greater discount down the line. We always point out our spotless reputation for reliability and transparency. When we make an agreement we do not try to move the goalposts or walk away unless a serious problem occurs. We always point out that the potential offer of a few extra thousand is not worth it for the loss of a guaranteed sale to a reputable and experienced company such as ourselves.

The valuation on the Leeds property came back at £68,500, so we were lucky. Because we'd agreed on a fixed price of £50,000 that actually meant we got a 27% discount. You may ask if we could have increased our offer slightly, but we'd taken a risk by agreeing to a fixed fee rather than a percentage (something we don't often do). We had actually protected ourselves against falling below a 23% discount by having a cut-off point at £65,000, i.e. if the valuation had come back at below £65,000 – which was quite possible – the deal was off. Although of course we would have made an immediate lower offer because we had still invested time and money into the project.

With the deal a "go", we instructed the solicitors and the conveyancing process began. It was all fairly straightforward. The only exceptional piece of documentation we needed beyond the usual was his mother's death certificate and proof that he was now the legal owner of the property, which we were able to get as probate had been completed. The deal went through in two months and the seller walked away from the property a happy man, with £50,000 in his pocket!

CHAPTER 12

Property With Registered Charges Against It In Stanmore

Around September 2014, a member of my property network passed along the details of a man who wanted a quick sale on a property in Stanmore, a suburb of northwest London. The area is fairly affluent and the property was a sizeable one. It was a four-bedroom detached house with a garage and a substantial garden.

When my negotiator spoke with the owner, she quickly established the fact that he wanted to sell the property because he wanted to pay off some loans and move to India, where he was originally from, to retire. He said he believed the property was worth around £700,000–750,000.

We started our due diligence and found a very similar property on his street that was on the market for £850,000. However, on closer inspection, we realized that the house had been on the market for six months, so that wasn't an accurate guideline. Admittedly the house was in need of a little cosmetic work (although it was definitely move-in ready), but the length of time it had been sitting on the market was a reason to be cautious about the valuation.

The seller took a long time to send over photos of his house. When we did finally receive them, we saw that the house looked to be in adequate condition; in fact it was very similar to the comparable property we'd looked at online. The décor was fine and it was move-in ready, but could have benefited from a little updating. As far as we could tell at this point, the valuation of £700,000–750,000 seemed plausible. Unfortunately the seller had now seen the price the neighbour's house was being marketed at and thought that would increase the value of his house. We told the seller that, in our opinion, the estate agent had inflated the value of his neighbour's house, explaining that London properties usually sold quite fast and the fact that it had not sold was an indication that it was overpriced. Furthermore, the neighbour's house was in slightly better condition than his house.

Finally we got the seller to see that his house was probably worth in the region of £750,000–780,000. We made him an offer of £650,000, based on us getting a valuation of at least £750,000. This gave us a discount of around 13%. (We do normally accept that we will get lower discounts on BMV deals on properties in this kind of price bracket, usually 12–15%.)

Once the price and terms of the deal had been agreed, we sent him a lock-out agreement. However, he didn't send it back for weeks. He kept calling to ask when the valuer was coming, and we kept explaining that we would not be sending the valuer until we got the paperwork – the signed lock-out agreement – back from him. At this point, with all her past experience, my negotiator said she was pretty sure the seller was withholding information. She's extremely good at reading people! So she started doing a little due diligence on the property and began by doing a title search. This is not something we would normally do up front (it is a basic search done during the conveyancing process), but on this occasion my negotiator had a hunch.

A title search will tell you if there are any claims on the property from creditors (people who are owed money that has been lent with the property acting as security for the loan). On this property we were fairly unsurprised to discover that there were four charges against it! Our seller had mentioned that he had some debts to pay off, but had failed mentioned that he was actually in *default* on them and the creditors had called in the loan, which meant that they had the right to get the property sold and claim the money owed to them out of the sale of the property. At one time people didn't realize how serious it was if they secured loans against the value of their property. These days you will always see "Your home may be at risk if you do not keep up payments on a loan secured against it" or similar wording on advertisements for credit cards and loans.

With the Stanmore property, we could see that four creditors had registered the debts with collection agencies, which meant that, as soon as the property was sold, a portion of the proceeds had to be given directly to the creditors. We had no idea how much these debts were for. It could have meant that there was no equity left in the property at all, as far as we knew.

We also noted that one of the creditors was a foreign company, so it was an overseas charge; this was not going to be a straightforward deal!

Finally, my negotiator confronted the seller about the debts. He said he hadn't mentioned them because he didn't think they were relevant. He believed that, once he got his money, he'd pay them off himself. He kept saying he had more than enough equity in the property. (He'd said that the mortgage was less than £10,000 and that the debts only amounted to around £50,000 in total.) However, he was still dragging his feet over the lock-out agreement. Eventually he admitted that he was scared to have yet another official claim on the property (even though it was a completely different situation). In the end (because we always try to be flexible and work with our sellers to find a solution that suits everyone) we got him to agree, in writing, that if we started the conveyancing process and he pulled out for any reason, he would reimburse our out-of-pocket expenses. Once we had this agreement in place, we instructed our solicitors. We also appointed a solicitor to act in the interests of the seller, so that we could be assured that things would move along swiftly.

The first thing the seller's solicitor had to do was to get a redemption certificate from each creditor showing the exact nature of their claim, including the full amount that was owed. We obviously needed written proof that the full amount of the debts did not eat into the money we would be receiving. We discovered that there was around £20,000 owed for a BMW, £14,000 to a loan company and just over £6,000 owed to the mortgage lender. The foreign company provided a letter to say that they would accept £20,000 to cover the outstanding debt.

The problem was that the law in the UK states that any debt owed to a foreign company secured on a property has to paid up in full *before* the property is sold, or you can't complete the sale. With UK companies, the debts can be paid off upon the sale of the property with the money being transferred by the acting solicitor, in the same way a mortgage is cleared off and the balance of funds go into the seller's account; but a foreign debt has to be paid off before the sale of the property can be finalized.

This was a huge spanner in the works, a real complication to the whole deal. We had absolutely no security. If we paid the £20,000 and then the sale fell through for any reason, we'd lose that money (because the seller didn't *have* any money; he'd also borrowed from his family and needed to pay them back too – his only asset was this house).

At this point, there were two solicitors working on this deal in the UK and the foreign company had also appointed a solicitor. That meant three solicitors were working to resolve the whole matter. Costs were mounting! However, we had also, at this stage, received a valuation from an estate agent of £780,000–800,000, which gave us a paper profit of £120,000–150,000, so it was still a deal well worth working at.

Christmas 2014 was now approaching and we had all been working on the deal for over two months. As well as the hold ups caused by trying to get three separate solicitors communicating efficiently, things were slowing down towards the end of the year. And then we were hit with yet another twist in the tale … we discovered that this foreign company that was owed the £20,000 had actually ceased trading and was in the hands of the Liberian authorities! It had been a solicitor working on behalf of the Liberian authorities who had made the offer of accepting £20,000 to wipe out the debt. However, in order to pay this off, the company had to be reinstated … at a cost of £15,000 (to someone)! As if this was not enough, a little further digging revealed that the sole director of this now-defunct company was … none other than *the seller himself!*

Obviously we thought carefully about continuing; at one point we definitely considered cutting our losses (knowing we were unlikely to see our expenses reimbursed by the seller as he had no liquid funds anyway) and walking away, but we'd come this far down the road, and on some level we simply didn't want to accept defeat. There is something satisfying, even over and above the profit you will make, in seeing a deal through to the end.

We battled on and tried to have direct communication with the Liberian authorities ourselves regarding the reinstatement fee of £15,000. We needed some kind of reassurance that if for any reason the reinstatement ended up being unsuccessful, the fee would be refundable. The seller gave us permission to negotiate directly with the Liberian authorities' solicitor through our solicitor. We also asked for proof that the seller was, indeed, the *sole* director. At this point we had nightmares of new directors coming out of the wood-work and laying claim to the company, which could have affected its potential reinstatement!

Just to recap where we stood at this point ... we were preparing to pay £15,000 to reinstate a company and then transfer £20,000 to it in settlement of the debt the seller owed it. We could *then* buy the property from the seller. Out of the proceeds, the seller's solicitor would pay off the UK creditors so that all charges on the property would be lifted.

At this point I was beginning to have concerns about the mental health of my top negotiator who was dealing with the whole drama!

The seller was also calling the office repeatedly, sometimes two or three times a day, asking when the whole deal was going to complete. It's sometimes hard to keep your cool when you are helping someone and they become particularly demanding!

Finally, we got written confirmation from the Liberian authorities that they would refund the £15,000 if, for any reason, the reinstatement of the company was unsuccessful. We were told that the reinstatement would take about four to six weeks to go through but there was no guarantee. Of course it was in their interests to get it pushed through as soon as they could as they were the receivers and they would then get reimbursed for the debt.

We carefully weighed up our options and finally decided that the risks were worth taking. At this point we were five months into the process. Finally, we decided to go for it.

Our solicitor advised us that the safest way forward was to exchange contracts on the property so that we were more secure than simply having the seller's written agreement to reimburse our expenses (which meant little given his financial situation). So we transferred the 10% deposit (£65,000) to the seller's solicitor. It was agreed that the £15,000 to reinstate the company and the £20,000 debt could be paid out of that. This was a much better way forward than for us to pay the money directly to the Liberian authorities, because technically it was coming out of the seller's money and we had the protection of having exchanged contracts, so our investment was safe.

With these quick BMV deals we normally exchange and complete simultaneously, but this was obviously a unique situation!

In the end it took only two weeks for the company to be reinstated and we completed the purchase of the property in March. The whole deal had taken six months. I think it was the longest deal we have ever been involved in!

This case clearly shows you that with these kinds of deals you must a) be highly persistent, b) be flexible and think on your feet and c) use all available resources and do whatever it takes. I am sure most people would have given up at the first hurdle, which is why I feel fortunate to have such experienced and resilient negotiators on my team!

13

Urgent Sale Needed To Clear Debts In Birmingham

One evening, just as my team was finishing up for the evening, a woman called the office. She'd got the number from our website. She said she really needed to speak to someone, so she was put through to one of our negotiators. She explained to him that she urgently needed to sell her one-bedroom flat to pay off some debts.

The flat was near Birmingham. She assured us that it was in excellent condition and close to amenities. She'd put it on the market with a couple of estate agents at £67,000, but was getting nervous because there hadn't been enough viewings. She said she'd seen our ad online and was hoping we could buy her flat as soon as possible. This was in November 2014 and the flat had already been on the market for three to four weeks. She was told that we would do a little research and call her back as soon as possible.

What was very interesting was that when my negotiator did his due diligence, he discovered that the woman had only bought the flat six months previously. When he called her back, he asked why she was selling it so soon. She cited the debts as her main reason, but people in that situation will usually move out and rent the property because they stand to lose money (in conveyancing fees and other costs) by selling after only owning the property for six months. Furthermore, we discovered that she had actually bought the flat for £69,000 so it seemed very strange that she was prepared to lose £2,000 on it. We were sure there was more to the story. Finally, she explained everything that had happened.

This woman had originally bought the flat outright using the settlement she'd received after a divorce. The reason she'd put all her money into the property was that she couldn't qualify for a mortgage. She had a history of mental health problems and hadn't been able to find anyone to lend to her. She'd had some money left over that she'd put into savings, but her ex-boyfriend had cheated her out of it all, run up debts in her name and had then disappeared. She said she wanted to sell up, pay off the debts and start afresh, by moving into rented accommodation with her new boyfriend.

Talking to her, my negotiator got the distinct impression that the woman was naïve and trusted too easily. It was a rather sad story. It was very clear that she could have had a very comfortable life in her mortgage-free property, living off her savings. Her illness meant that she couldn't work, so this would have made her very comfortable. She'd obviously made a very bad choice in her ex-boyfriend and it was a real shame she was suffering such difficult consequences.

We wanted to help her, but the most we could offer her was £55,000 based on a valuation of £65,000 (which was only a 15% discount for us but we really felt sorry for this woman). We knew we would never get the valuation back up to £69,000 because the estate agent had put the property on the market at £67,000 and no valuer will value a property at higher than it has been on the market for. Plus, as she hadn't got offers when it was on the market at £67,000, we had to assume it was worth closer to £65,000. We nevertheless knew that the property was a good investment. It was in a good area and was in excellent condition. There were quite a few new builds in the area and it was a highly rentable property. We also knew that the market in the area was on the up. It really was a crying shame that she had to sell because it would have been a nice nest egg for her.

As much as I have to run a business, there are times when I feel I have to be more compassionate than usual, and this was one of those times. In fact, we tried to persuade her to keep hold of the property and rent it out, but she was adamant she wanted to sell. (This would have been an ideal case for a sale and rent back deal back in the day before legislation made it virtually impossible.)

Eventually she agreed in principle to our offer but said she just wanted to give the property one more chance with the estate agent over the weekend to see if she could get the full asking price. My negotiator promised to give the woman a call on the Monday. When he did, the woman said she'd had some more viewings but no offers.

She was still holding out hope one of the people who viewed over the weekend would make an offer. We told her that our offer was still on the table but that she had to make a decision fairly quickly because she was in an urgent situation. If she didn't release the equity or rent the place out soon, she would default on her debt repayments.

The woman agreed to the lock-out agreement. My negotiator emailed it to her, asking her to print it out, sign it and have it witnessed and then to send it back. However, after a couple of days, he hadn't heard from her. He started calling her, but every time he did it went to voice mail. After a few days, he assumed she'd changed her mind. However, he tried one more time. He happened to call from his own mobile phone rather than the office number and this time she picked up – so obviously she'd been avoiding his calls.

The seller apologized for not being available, explaining that her medication made her drowsy so she'd been sleeping a lot. She said she hadn't heard the phone on the other occasions he'd called. This is typical of people in a highly stressful situation; they tend to bury their heads in the sand. My negotiator said to her, gently, "Look, my job is to help you, not just to make money, so tell me, what is really bothering you?"

Finally she told him that she was worried that it was all happening too fast and she didn't have somewhere to move to. She'd found a property she liked but she didn't have the money to put a deposit down so she'd lost it. She also knew that, because she wasn't working, it would be difficult to pass a rental agency's credit check. (Who knows what had happened to the new boyfriend!)

My negotiator reassured her and explained to her that the sooner the sale went through, the sooner she would have that lump sum and be able to negotiate favourably with rental agents, perhaps offering to pay six months' rent up front as security.

I hope I'm showing here how important it is to build a personal relationship with the seller. You can't really help them fully unless you get to the bottom of what's going on and how they're feeling. People suffering from stress will often hide their real reasons for hesitation, and this could adversely affect their chance to move on and release themselves from a responsibility that they can no longer handle, the one thing that is causing them all the stress.

Many property investors get fixated on the offer and the money they stand to gain, but what is more important than anything is **understanding the seller's circumstances**. Unless the seller can see that there is a way out, that there is a real solution to their problems, they will be paralysed.

This need to focus on the human side of the story is the backbone of everything I want to say in the book … that this is the **new way of doing property deals**. This is a **people business** first and foremost.

My negotiator said to this woman, "I wish you'd told me about your worries sooner, because I would have reassured you that you were doing the right thing; you wouldn't have had to avoid my calls." He offered to go and meet her to answer all her questions and get the paperwork signed. He actually ended up having a terrible journey. It was a five-hour round trip to Birmingham from Milton Keynes (usually an hour or so each way) because of some extensive road works. He spent two hours with this woman, going through all the paperwork and answering all her questions. We'd jumped the gun and already instructed the solicitors, so they had also sent her some paperwork to sign. She needed to provide proof of her ID and address, and fill in some basic forms. But eventually he got everything signed and all the paperwork was in order.

It was very obvious that this woman was deeply disturbed by the experience she'd had of her ex-boyfriend cheating her out of all her money. She was nervous on the phone and my negotiator resorted to texting her through the conveyancing process, which she seemed more responsive too. This is another example of how you must know and understand your seller's needs and emotional state. Admittedly we don't rush off around the country to meet every seller, but because of her illness this woman was a special case. We needed to build a very close rapport with her.

Just before the sale went through she called to say that she had found somewhere to live. She was anxious about the sale because she needed some money to pay the holding fee for the rental property. There had been some holdups on her sale because it was a leasehold property and we were waiting for information from the management company. We paid the reservation fee for her. Then it transpired that she'd signed a three-month lock-out agreement with the estate agent that she obviously had to break. There was a £150 penalty fee so we paid that, too, to speed things up!

Finally the sale went through, we completed, she got her money and everyone was relieved and happy.

You can see that this deal was never about the actual figure on a piece of paper – that can always fluctuate no matter what you think you can get. What this deal was always about was the seller's desperate need to pay off the ex-boyfriend's debts that were in her name, and then find a safe and secure place to live. It was the understanding that these elements were the priority that helped us help her and ensure everyone came out with what they wanted and needed. A win-win situation!

CHAPTER

14

From BMV To Lease-Option Deal
In Liverpool

This case is a great example of how you have to know your situation and which tool to apply to it. This deal started as a straightforward BMV deal but we ended up needing a lease-option deal to complete it.

In July 2014, the female owner of this three-bedroom terrace house in a nice, convenient area of Liverpool was looking to sell up because she had relocated to Anglesey in Wales. She'd been renting the property out for some time (it was close to the university, so she had a good market with the student population) but was finding it increasingly difficult to manage. Since her last tenants had left, she hadn't had time to find new ones, so the property was standing empty and she saw this as her chance to sell. She'd been advised by her estate agent that the property was worth in the region of £85,000 based on comparable properties in the area, but had asked them to price it for a "quick sale" so they'd put the property on the market for £75,000 hoping it would attract people.

She'd had no offers from the estate agent and was struggling to maintain the monthly mortgage payments without her rental income. Eventually she called my company looking for a quick sale.

We did our due diligence on the property and it looked to be in good condition and was, indeed, in a good area. The problem was, we couldn't get a valuation of £85,000 because, as I explained before, once an estate agent has marketed a property at a certain price, no RICS (Royal Institute of Chartered Surveyors) valuer will come back with a valuation above that price. Thus we could only base our offer on a valuation of £75,000. We offered her 20% BMV, which was £60,000. As her outstanding mortgage was £68,000, there was no way she could accept the offer as that would not leave her with enough equity to pay off the mortgage.

This woman had literally devalued her own property ... it was a harsh lesson for her. If she wanted to sell the property and have enough money to pay off the mortgage and pay all her fees, she would have to hold out for the current full asking price of £75,000. No cash investor was going to give her that, her best bet was to find a first-time buyer who was not in a chain. But even then, the buyer may have tried to strike a deal. It was beginning to look like there was no way she could get any profit out of this house and that, once she covered all her fees, she was probably going to take a loss.

One of my negotiators talked through all of these factors with her. The woman said she was simply desperate to get rid of the property so she didn't have to pay the mortgage anymore. This was a perfect scenario to suggest a lease-option deal.

We explained to her that, under the terms of a lease-option deal, we would take over the mortgage payments and the maintenance of the property; we would manage the property and find tenants. In exchange, we would have the option to buy the property at an agreed price over a long period of time.

The mortgage was an interest only mortgage so it was fairly low, around £240 a month I think. As the capital sum would still be outstanding at the end of the mortgage term, which had 19 years left on it, our offer was £68,000. Obviously the value of the property was likely to go up considerably in 19 years, but we still took on that risk.

The woman sounded interested in the deal and was very keen to get the matter settled, which we said we could do in around three to four weeks. However, after a couple of days, she emailed us with a number of concerns. She said she had heard horror stories of what had happened to other people who had accepted similar deals. (As I have said before, there will always be unscrupulous people in this industry who will threaten to give the rest of us a bad name!) She had three major concerns.

Firstly, she'd heard a story of a property owner who had entered into a lease-option deal and then suddenly got a letter from the lender saying the mortgage hadn't been paid for three years and they were now liable for arrears and a repossession order was being prepared. We explained that this was an impossible story for a start, because no lender in the world would wait *three years* before serving you notice! So this story was a little dubious on this point alone. But we reassured her that it would be a legitimate watertight deal she would be entering into and that, although we would be taking over the mortgage payments, she should still monitor the mortgage and ensure the payments were processed every month. We would be legally bound to make all those payments. If even one payment was missed, for any reason, she would be able to sue us for breach of contract, recover any losses from us, and we would lose our option (which we would be unlikely to want to do after investing in the property).

Next, she was concerned about what would happen if the renters (that we would find) damaged the property in any way. She was worried that she might be liable for that damage. Again, we assured her that we would become legally responsible for the property, so we would be liable for all works in the property, just as an owner would be. The contract would literally make us assume all her legal responsibilities on the property. We would naturally take a deposit from any tenants we found, and manage the property in the usual way.

Finally, the seller asked about the buildings insurance. She wanted to know who was responsible for this. We explained that this would also be our responsibility. Either we could pay directly or she would pay and we would reimburse her. Either way, it would be stipulated in the contract that we were responsible for paying the buildings insurance.

The woman was happy with all these answers and finally it looked like we were getting somewhere. But she had one more request. She said that she was not willing to walk away with absolutely nothing after 19 years. As the value of the property was likely to have gone up considerably by then, she wanted to benefit a modest amount from that. So she wanted to agree on a fixed price of £85,000. Considering the property might be worth three to four times that in 19 years time (although you still have to adjust that for inflation), we felt it was a fair request; you don't always have to squeeze every drop out of a deal. I feel it's reasonable and ethical to give the seller a percentage of your future profit if you feel it would sweeten the deal.

Finally, the seller signed the lock-out agreement giving us time to get the lease-option deal together. We instructed solicitors and went back and forth on the paperwork. To be honest, it took longer than we expected because the seller didn't return the paperwork promptly (citing the fact she was away on a lot of courses), but we got there in the end. In total the whole process took three months. We finally exchanged contracts, part of which is a transfer of deeds that the seller has pre-signed, and we had our lease-option deal in place. Then we instructed our management company, got renters in, and all has gone smoothly.

CHAPTER 15

Urgent Lease-Option Deal In Lincoln

This case is very similar to the previous one. In this case, the seller had a nice two-bedroom house in Lincoln that she had bought while her son had been at university there; he'd lived in it and they'd rented out the second bedroom. She wanted an urgent sale because she was a nurse and was going out to Sierra Leone to help out in the ebola crisis that broke out in the summer of 2014. She had no idea how long she'd be there for and she didn't want to leave the property for her son and husband to take care of; she just wanted to be released from the responsibility of the property.

The house had gone on the market with an estate agent for £82,000. Her outstanding mortgage was £79,000, so there wasn't much equity in it. She really needed to sell at the asking price just to break even (once she'd paid the conveyancing fees). Our due diligence told us that the house was in a great street, very popular with students, so it was a good investment. However, the estate agents hadn't managed to get any interest. So she had called my company in a pretty desperate state. She was leaving for Sierra Leone imminently so she needed to sort the matter out urgently.

My negotiator explained to this woman that we couldn't base our offer on anything more than the £82,000 the property had been marketed at, and that meant we could only offer £64,000 (around 20% BMV). This would not even have paid off the woman's mortgage, so this was not an option for her. She only had three and a half weeks before she left for Sierra Leone. There was no way she'd be able to sell the house on the open market in that time, so she was pretty desperate by this point. She did say that, worst case scenario, she could leave the country and let her husband and son take care of renting out the property, but this was not her preference; she was very nervous that if she was out of the country they would not be able to cope if problems occurred because neither of them had any experience of managing the rented property. She really wanted to be rid of the responsibility.

At this point, my negotiator pitched a lease-option deal to her. She immediately got the concept and knew it was the right thing for her. The situation was very similar to that of the lady in Liverpool. The mortgage was an interest-only mortgage (as is usual with buy-to-let mortgages, which both of these were) and she had about 18 years left on it. This time, she mentioned up front that she'd need a sweetener, so we went straight in with an offer of £85,000; after all, we knew that she had one more option (to leave her husband and son in charge of the property) even if it was her last resort. She was walking away from £200–250 in rental income (that would now come to us) so we knew we needed to offer her something more, an incentive to move forward with us. This way, when we bought the property under our option, she would get £6,000 after she paid off her mortgage capital of £69,000.

We came to an agreement and I told our solicitors that the deal *had* to be done in three and a half weeks. Thankfully, with our excellent relationship with our experienced solicitor, we were able to expedite the process and we managed to get all the paperwork signed just before she left. (This is a great example of why you need great relationships … if we hadn't had such a good relationship with our solicitor, I doubt the deal would have been done in time.)

What I really like about this story is that it isn't about someone utterly desperate. She simply wanted to get her affairs tied up before moving on to a new stage in her life, before a big change took place. She was particularly sharp and intelligent; a very savvy lady who didn't get paranoid about an unconventional deal. As I say, she understood the concept quickly and saw why it was an excellent choice for her. We didn't really have to *sell* the idea to her; the concept sold itself … as it does to smart people! And as a result, because she was rather savvy, she got a little more out of it than we usually offer.

16

Lease-Option Deal On Dilapidated Property In Sheffield

In early 2015, we were approached by a man who wanted a quick sale on his three-bedroom property in Sheffield. He'd put it on the market for £75,000, but it had sat there for a while and he'd received no offers. When we looked at the property on the website, it was obvious why. The place had been completely trashed and needed a total refurbishment. Sadly, while the owner had been living in Manchester, his tenants in Sheffield had completely wrecked the place and then left it empty. It was subsequently broken into and stripped bare. All the copper pipes had been ripped out and taken, windows had been removed, and as the thieves had made their getaway they had completely demolished the garden fence. Even the walls had been damaged in places, so there was plastering work to be done.

This is the kind of seller I feel particularly sorry for. He was stuck. He didn't have the money to do the necessary work to bring the house up to a reasonable standard, and it was obvious he was going to find it very difficult to sell it in the state it was in. The property had great potential and had obviously been in a good state before the former tenants had trashed it; it was in an area of Sheffield that was popular with students so it was a good investment in the long term.

The owner had already received a quote from a builder of £7,400 to do up the whole house, but when we looked closely at it, we estimated that it would take at least another £2,000 because the quote didn't include flooring and rewiring, which we knew would be needed. We estimated that the total cost of the refurbishment would be closer to £10,000.

The mortgage on this property was a repayment one (i.e. interest plus capital) and the outstanding amount was £80,000, so he was already prepared to sell at a slight loss, but there was no way he could have accepted a BMV offer from us as all we could have offered was £60,000 (20% below the estate agent's listed price of £75,000). Thus we were left with a potential lease-option deal. He was very receptive to it and we sent him a three-month lock-out agreement.

Weeks went by and he didn't get back to us; we began to wonder if he was stringing us along, but he told us that the estate agent had got several viewings, so we could see that it was the estate agent getting his hopes up. When the promised offers never materialized, he realized he had two choices. Either he borrowed more money to do the refurbishment and then had another go at selling the property through the estate agent, or he went with our lease-option deal.

Our due diligence had revealed a similar property on the same street that had sold for £67,000. Admittedly it was two-bedroom house, which was one less than our seller's property, but it was in excellent condition. This told us that our seller's place was possibly only worth £55,000–60,000, so he was already in serious negative equity.

Once we laid out the stark facts to our seller, he really understood that in reality our offer was his only option.

The remaining mortgage term was 21 years. We offered to pay £80,000, which was the remaining mortgage balance at that time. He countered our first offer by asking for a further £8,000 at the time we exercised our option and completed the same, plus an upfront fee of £1,000 when we made the deal. We knew we'd be getting a decent rental income for 21 years and there would be a sizeable amount of equity in the property by then, so it wasn't a completely unreasonable request. However, we still needed to get our own quote for the necessary renovation work. We sent a builder up to look at the property and he came back with a quote of £15,000, and that was just to get the property back up to a *liveable* standard! This blew our budget out of the water, so we had to go back to the negotiating table.

The seller was adamant that our builder had over-quoted for the work. In the end he found a local builder with an excellent reputation who came back with a quote for £6,300. This was acceptable, but we still felt that the £8,000 the seller wanted on completion of the sale was high. We ended up agreeing on £5,000. Then there was the issue of the £1,000 fee he wanted up front. We weren't happy to pay that on top, given how much we would be spending on the renovation. The seller offered to travel to Sheffield regularly and oversee the renovation work (taking and sending us photos and progress reports, etc.), and suggested we pay him a fee for that. This wasn't a bad idea, but we offered him £600, which he accepted.

Finally we were ready to sign all the paperwork, but the whole process had taken so long and there had been so much time wasting going on that, although the seller had signed an original three-month lock-out agreement in February 2015, we actually had to go back to him and get a second agreement in May!

I'm pleased to say that the seller was as good as his word and travelled regularly to the house to oversee the works and send us progress reports and photos. Once it was finished, the house was transformed and we were able to rent it out quickly.

One thing we learnt from this deal is that it always pays to get several quotes for a piece of work, and especially to find a reputable local builder as they get good deals on the resources they need. If you bring in a builder from elsewhere, they also have to factor travel and accommodation costs into their quote.

CHAPTER 17

Part Now, Part Later Deal On Probate Property In Barnsley

The sellers in this case came to us through our website in the summer of 2013. They were a brother and sister who had inherited a two-bedroom flat in Barnsley from their mother when she passed away. They had put it on the market with an estate agent, but there was no interest so they quickly took it off. They wanted a quick sale to release the equity in the property.

Our due diligence confirmed that comparable flats were worth £110,000, the estimate they'd suggested, so we offered £82,500, which was a 25% discount. However, when we looked more closely at the property we realized that it was in need of some modernization. Also a similar property on the block was lingering on the market at £110,000. In the end we offered them £80,000, which they accepted, *but* the valuation came back even lower than we expected, at £95,000, so with a 25% discount all we could offer them was £71,250. They were understandably upset. There was no mortgage on the property, but they said they didn't want to feel as though they were giving it away.

Finally, we said we would pay them £71,250 immediately, and a further £5,000 in five years time (estimating that there would be an additional £5,000 capital appreciation in five years time), giving them a total of £76,250 for the property, which represented a fraction over 20% BMV on the valuation of £95,000.

They accepted the deal on condition that the £5,000 was documented as a loan to us, secured by a charge on the property that we would allow them to register. We accepted that on condition that they pre-sign a document that lifted the charge as soon as the £5,000 was confirmed as having been paid. (You need to submit this paperwork to the land registry in order to get the charge lifted, so we didn't want the possibility of any delays. There are quite stringent security measures around charges on properties.)

After this, it was a fairly straightforward process of getting proof that they were joint beneficiaries of their mother's property. Everything had to be signed by both parties so it took slightly longer than usual, but there were no glitches; everything went through smoothly. We finally completed the purchase in November 2013.

One month after we bought the property, a similar flat in the block sold for £100,000, so we could see prices were climbing back up. In the summer of 2015, just under two years later, we did a home track valuation on the property and the estimated value was £102,000, so I'm confident we will be able to take out the £5,000 to give them in November 2018.

CHAPTER 18

The Dutch Deals

Since 2013, I have been working closely with an associate in the Netherlands. I thought it would be interesting to share some of the deals we have done there. I met this extraordinary woman at a property seminar in 2012. We formed a friendship and eventually went into business together. What immediately struck me about her was her genuine commitment to add value to people's lives. She knew that she could help herself by helping others. This was very much in tune with my ethos, and I have always found her to have the highest standards and codes of ethics, so it has been a joy working with her.

The property business in Holland is a very different animal to the business in the UK. The Dutch system is extremely autocratic; there is almost a cartel between the five big banks in Holland. In good times they loaned money irresponsibly; during the bad times they repossessed ruthlessly. And it seemed that there was little that the people could do about it.

One of the biggest problems in Holland is getting banks to give homeowners consent to let. In the UK, lenders have to give a pretty good reason to refuse consent to let; in Holland it's almost a blanket refusal, you have to work hard to get permission. Even if you get consent, it is usually only for five years and they can turn around and revoke it after the first year! In the UK we would be up in arms if banks behaved like this, but in Holland it's hard to protest when everything seems to be controlled by five big banks, like big bullies!

The Dutch people definitely have a sense of injustice, but they seem to be reluctant to speak out against it. There seems to be a cultural reluctance to complain. I've spoken to some people who say they feel like they are "in chains". The government is no help. Unfortunately, there has historically been a big problem with people laundering money through the Dutch property market. They would "wash" black money by buying houses with cash and then selling them quickly. But for me, a challenge is like a red rag to a bull. Tell me I can't do something and I will find a way I can. That's the entrepreneurial spirit. Entrepreneurs do three things: they 1) create opportunities, 2) raise money and 3) solve problems. Many people blame their environment or "the system" for getting in the way of things they want to do. But entrepreneurs love working their way around challenges; it's a game, we get a buzz when we figure out a way to win!

While you can apply the investment strategies we've already discussed in this book in the Netherlands, there are some limitations and in some cases you have to go about things in a slightly different way. However, the Golden Rules still apply. You always deal directly with motivated sellers, you focus on negotiating the terms as well as the price, you make sure you are offering a win-win deal and you always act ethically.

One of the trickiest strategies to apply in Holland, of course, is lease-options. Yet they are desperately needed, as over a million homes are currently in negative equity in the Netherlands. We have to look for every loop hole possible to get the bank to consent to let. And even when we can, as I explained, we can often only get that short-term approval of five years, rather than the 15–20 years you can do a lease-option deal for in the UK. You can still do an HMO (House of Multiple Occupancy), but only if you bought in cash. You can also flip a deal, with person A buying a house from person C, in a deal sourced by person B (who gets a share of the profit). But generally there is a great deal of red tape when it comes to property investing compared to other countries.

The easiest strategy to use is BMV, to help people release the equity from properties, especially when they own them outright without a mortgage. We have come across many elderly people keen to sell for 75% of the value of their home just to release the equity. And there is a way of doing a type of sale and rent back deal, although we can't call it that!

My business partner in Holland has a very interesting background. She grew up in a small town outside Rotterdam. She studied

Facilities Management at university and then did an MBA. This took her to the public health sector. She worked in administration and supply chain logistics for the Dutch health care system. On one level, I suppose this gave her a love of helping people. This was one of the first qualities that I identified in her … that she was a *people person*. This is critical for our business.

She was well rewarded within her field, once earning the title of "manager of the year", so I knew she also had excellent organizational and managerial skills. She had travelled extensively and this seemed to have given her strong self-confidence and an open-minded, balanced outlook. She also had some experience of commercial property – from the time when she worked in elderly care and was involved in changing a building from a public-funded estate to a commercial enterprise – and had bought a few investment properties for cash. For all these reasons and more, I knew she was going to be an excellent business partner for me.

It took us almost a year to set up our property investment business in the Netherlands. The bank account alone took six months to open, because we were a UK-registered limited company. We had to get all the forms and contracts written in both English and Dutch, and the translations notarized. It was a nightmare, but worth it in the end as business has been so successful. Our first deal (not the greatest we've done but it helped boost our moral) closed in April 2014 and since then we have not looked back. We try to focus on BMV deals because lease-option deals are only possible if there isn't too much negative equity, but we still consider everything because … we love a challenge!

A Bad Bank!

One of the earlier deals we got involved with shows just how the property market and banks act against the population in Holland.

We were contacted by a man who said he was desperate to move house. He was a married police officer with two young children. He had been threatened in his home by a released criminal seeking revenge, so they were feeling particularly uncomfortable in their own home. He was in a negative equity situation so he couldn't sell up on the open market without taking a loss and owing money he didn't have; a lease-option deal was clearly the only way forward.

Our first move was to contact the bank to try and get permission for the seller to rent out the property. We knew we couldn't do anything without that. We waited and waited, and the bank never came back to us. Eventually the seller moved out, rented a new place for his family and leased out his own property illegally to cover the rent in the new place. He was actually about six months behind in his mortgage payments, too. More than a year went by before the bank made contact … and it was not to give the seller permission to let, it was to call in the arrears! But this guy had nothing; he couldn't pay his debts. To make matters worse, he had also lost his job; he was in a really bad way.

Eventually the bank took the man to court and threatened to repossess the property and sell it via an auction. At this point, we found out that the bank had originally written to this man to try and get his written permission for them to put the house on the open market. But the man was a joint owner with his wife and the wife had flatly refused to sign the agreement. She had been frightened that they would lose their home. However, they had now ended up in a very bad situation. They had mounting debts, the man was unemployed and they had an illegal tenant in their house.

My business partner went with the man to court and explained his whole story. She explained how the man had tried his best to get permission from the bank to rent out his property. She also explained how disgusted she was with the bank's treatment of this homeowner. She told an interesting story about how the contact at the bank had ended up a contact in her LinkedIn network, so she'd written directly to him to ask what on earth had been going on. He told her a sob story about his wife being sick and then dying. Her response, quite correctly, had been: "That's very sad and I'm sorry for you, but that is irrelevant to this case!" She told the court that she'd subsequently made a formal complaint at the bank.

Interestingly, the bank did not send a member of staff to the court case (probably arrogantly assuming the case would automatically be ruled in their favour), only their lawyer was present, so the judge actually started to become sympathetic to the man's case. When this guy got up in court and basically said, "I've been a police officer since I began working, I've defended the lives of the people in this country with my own life, and this is how I am treated?" the judge completely came down on his side, saying that she could see too many strange things going on with the bank's behaviour. She ordered a review of the case and asked the bank to come back with a fairer deal. She could see that a lease-option deal would be a good solution; the monthly mortgage would get paid and the house could be sold after a couple of years without any debt.

The bank took its time to come back to us, during which time the man was at least able to get some police compensation for being unable to work due to stress. Finally the bank came back with the idea of giving the man's debt to a debt manager, which hardly addressed all the problems on the table. It was a terrible proposal!

All this man really wanted to do was to go back to Morocco, where he was originally from, and disappear. He was broken and burnt out. He had lost all confidence in himself and could not bear to tell his children, who were aged five and seven, that he had failed them.

In the end, the bank forced the man out of his house, making him effectively homeless and facing a €30,000 debt. The bank was ruthless when there was a perfectly acceptable win-win situation on the table. No, they wanted to win their way, no matter if they put a man and his family out on the street with a crippling debt.

Turkish Delight!

This next story is one of my personal favourites (and the one I referred to in an earlier chapter). My Dutch business partner was in The Hague when she was contacted by some people who'd seen her ad online. She normally did all her deals over the phone, but the property was very near where she was heading for a meeting so she decided to go and see this couple who said they were in dire straits.

When she arrived at the property, she found a female owner sitting on the steps outside, utterly dejected. The story was that this woman was due to move back to Turkey, where her husband was already based. They'd got a buyer for the house, they'd moved out into a temporary place, sold all their furniture, taken their children out of the schools ... they had both already quit their jobs in the Netherlands; they were ready and waiting to go. But that's when the buyer dropped out suddenly, claiming he couldn't get the financing together. It was a little naïve to have sold all their furniture and moved before the sale went through, but that just made my business partner want to help them even more, so she suggested a lease-option deal.

Now came our dreaded next move ... applying to the bank for permission to let. Usually, in Holland, you apply to the council first;

if they give their permission, then you go to the bank, and they usually say no! Even if they say yes, they force you to pay an outside company to process the mountains of paperwork they require. This company never visits the property; they just pick an arbitrary figure out of the air and charge you a fee for a whole year, basically for doing the work that a lettings agency would normally do, but without finding you the renters! Or they won't find suitable renters, or will not negotiate the correct rent that you need. When we explained we didn't *need* them to do this work, they said fine, but we had to pay a compensation fee to them. When we asked why, they explained that they would lose out on an administration fee they charge to renters and the commission they could collect on the monthly rent! Only when we made a serious complaint to the bank did they back down.

The paperwork for this deal was a bit ridiculous, but we did finally get the consent to let and completed the lease-option deal with the Turkish couple, who were then reunited in Turkey. They were so profoundly grateful they put a glowing testimonial on our website and extended an open invitation to us if we ever want to visit Turkey!

Sadly though, this story did not quite end there. A year later, the bank was on the phone asking why the property was not yet sold. We explained to them that it was because the property was still in negative equity, and pointed out that we had their consent to let for five years. It's a formal condition of the agreement that you should put the property on the market (which we always do, but obviously for a price that covers the mortgage and costs). For three months we kept talking to the bank trying to convince them there was no need to sell the property this year because the market was picking up and we would be able to sell without occurring a debt in a couple of years. But at the beginning of 2016, the bank forced us to sell, threatening to revoke the consent to let if we didn't! We couldn't be left with a property on which we had to pay a monthly mortgage but couldn't let out ... so we were forced to sell at a loss. Not the happiest of endings!

*   *   *

I was attracted to doing business in Holland precisely *because* of the stringent rules there. Part of me wanted to help fight the injustice, to give the people their voice. There is no good reason for the system to be as autocratic as it is. We all know the law has to change; I want to be a part of that. We go in using guerrilla tactics. We are building a system to try and bypass the banks and work directly with private equity companies and significant investors. We've already made some big waves by getting our first lease-option deals legitimized. However, the challenges we faced were so complex that we've decided to use different strategies in Holland. For example, we have started to do sale and rent back deals (which are not feasible in the UK anymore). We are also championing a property fund to give investors another way of getting a return from property investment. Certain strategies are better suited to certain countries because of their different rules.

Of course, with things the way they are, when we do a good deal in the Netherlands the added reward is the extreme gratitude of people when we find them a solution for what they had assumed was an impossible situation!

Final Word: The Future Of The Property Business – Your Role

When I first start talking to people about the strategies outlined in this book, they always say, "But who would do that?" I explain that lots of people would and *have*. Indeed, I am in business with many of them! I have experienced these strategies as an investor, as a landlord *and* as a tenant. Indeed, at the time of writing I am playing all three roles: I am a landlord with rent-to-buy tenants in my properties, I am a mortgage host *and* I am a rent-to-buy tenant.

The bottom line is this: ordinary people with ordinary salaries can no longer get onto the property ladder. I've explained why this is several times throughout the course of this book; I've shown how the figures simply don't add up. The *only* way ordinary people with ordinary salaries (who have not inherited cash or been given a lump sum to invest in property by family or friends) can get onto the property ladder is to treat property like a business and raise capital from investors in order to start this business.

I believe that everyone deserves to know what is available to them, otherwise they are operating under "unconscious incompetence", i.e. not knowing what they don't know. Or as Donald Rumsfeld put it: "There are known knowns. These are things we know that we know. There are known unknowns. That is to say, there are things that we know we don't know. But there are also *unknown unknowns*. There are things we don't know we don't know."

Now you know what you know, you have a responsibility to take this information to other people. Your role is to learn how to use these strategies and then teach them to others, so that everyone has a fair chance if they want to better their lives.

The property business is *not* for the faint hearted. But for the strong hearted it can be exceptionally rewarding. However, you have to be prepared to take risks. Most people are unable to do this. If you speak to an ordinary person and say, "Hey, I am going to ask you to work harder than you've ever worked, but I will *only* pay you based on your results. Plus, you will get no holiday, you will work longer hours than all your friends, you'll have to do another job to bring in money to pay the bills, you'll get a hard time from many other people, especially friends and family, you'll have to beg for funds and still pay the tax man ..." most people would run a mile and ask, "Who the hell would *do* that?!" I say ... **entrepreneurs**!

Most people are raised to stay in a very safe zone. They want that guaranteed pay cheque. If they – or someone they know – has never experienced something, they think it can't be done. There is a chasm between the way regular people in the rat race think, and the way entrepreneurial business people think. This is *not* for everyone ... this will cause you stress and make you scared, you will lose sleep, you will probably lose friends (who don't believe you are doing the right thing because it is "outside of the box"), but the rewards might be huge. If you want to guarantee that you sleep well at night, have no worries, never feel fear, always feel in control, then *don't do this*! Get a regular job, get your pay cheque, have a fear-free life, but *don't complain* and say you want more! Be happy with your lot. I listen to people all the time who tell me their goals and dreams ... but they are not willing to do what it takes.

Everything you have read in this book could radically change your life. But most people, even when they've read this book, won't do it.

Is there any guarantee of success? No. But you can give yourself the **best chance** at success by doing the work, doing the research, reading the book, and then *practising*!

I'm showing you a choice ... a path for you to follow. If security is paramount to you then it would be insane to do this, but if you want to grow and excel, and have a chance at the best rewards possible, then go for it!

The rewards are always better than anything you can currently imagine. You think you can imagine driving an Aston Martin? Let me tell you, the reality is *much* better than you can imagine. You think you can imagine travelling around the world First Class? Believe me, it is beyond anything you could dream up. However ... the flip side is that the pain, when things don't go to plan, is *worse* than anything you can imagine. You think you can imagine being broke, or losing £100,000? I promise you, you can't. You can't imagine what it feels like to wake up in a cold sweat at 3am, realizing you are not having a bad dream, that the nightmare is your reality and that you have hell to face in the morning. I can tell you that with every pain barrier you go through, the pain lessens. As you get older and more experienced, the pain diminishes, but the first time you go through it, it truly is *hell*!

So it's up to you: if you can face the pain, you'll get the gain; if you can't, you won't ... but that's okay. We are all different.

If you do go for it, remember what Winston Churchill said:

"Never, never, never give up."

Index